Gene
THERAPY

Medical
Marvels

Medical
Marvels

Gene
THERAPY
by L. E. Carmichael

Content Consultant

Nathaniel Comfort, PhD
Associate Professor
Institute of the History of Medicine
The John Hopkins University

Credits

Published by ABDO Publishing Company, PO Box 398166, Minneapolis, MN 55439. Copyright © 2014 by Abdo Consulting Group, Inc. International copyrights reserved in all countries. No part of this book may be reproduced in any form without written permission from the publisher. The Essential Library™ is a trademark and logo of ABDO Publishing Company.

Printed in the United States of America,
North Mankato, Minnesota
062013
092013

 THIS BOOK CONTAINS AT LEAST 10% RECYCLED MATERIALS.

Editor: Rebecca Felix
Series Designer: Craig Hinton

Photo credits: Benjamin Albiach Galan/Shutterstock Images, cover; Shutterstock Images, cover, 23; R. Gino Santa Maria/Shutterstock Images, cover; Stephen Voss, 7; Zhabska Tetyana/Shutterstock Images, 8; iStockphoto/Thinkstock, 12, 81; Time Life Pictures/Mansell/Time Life Pictures/Getty Images, 17; Red Line Editorial, 18, 33, 54, 66, 79, 85; BSIP/UIG/Getty Images, 20; Alila Sao Mai/Shutterstock Images, 26, 43; Hemera/Thinkstock, 29; Sakuma/AP Images, 35; John Harding/Time Life Pictures/Getty Images, 39; Adam Howard/DK Images, 41; Ted Thai/Time Life Pictures/Getty Images, 47; Marianne Barcellona/Time Life Pictures/Getty Images, 51; Mark Duncan/AP Images, 55; Douglas Graham/Congressional Quarterly/Getty Images, 58; Raphael Gaillarde/Gamma-Rapho/Getty Images, 61, 73; Science Picture Co/Science Faction/SuperStock, 63; Daniel Hulshizer/AP Images, 69; Athanasia Nomikou/Shutterstock Images, 87; Cultura/Liam Norris/Getty Images, 91; Princeton University/AP Images, 95; Adam Gault/Getty Images, 99

Library of Congress Control Number: 2013932975
Cataloging-in-Publication Data

Carmichael, L. E.
 Gene therapy / L. E. Carmichael.
  p. cm. -- (Medical marvels)
Includes bibliographical references and index.
ISBN 978-1-61783-902-3
1. Gene therapy--Juvenile literature. I. Title.
615.8--dc23

2013932975

Contents

The Boy Who Could Not See

Corey Haas was a happy baby, but something was definitely wrong. "He wasn't reaching for things right in front of him, like other babies do," said his mother Nancy.[1] Corey only played with toys that were lying in bright sunlight, and he was fascinated by glowing lightbulbs, staring at them much longer than most people can.

Corey's vision worsened as he grew. By the time he started school, he used a cane to help him avoid objects in his path and needed special reading equipment. "If Corey was in a typical classroom where the kids would find the light bright enough to read, he could not," said Corey's doctor, Jean Bennett. "His pupils would dilate as far as they could, as if they were trying to pull every photon out of the room."[2]

Corey's sight-assisting cane rests against him as he holds a video game close in order to make out the screen in 2008.

Photoreceptor Cells

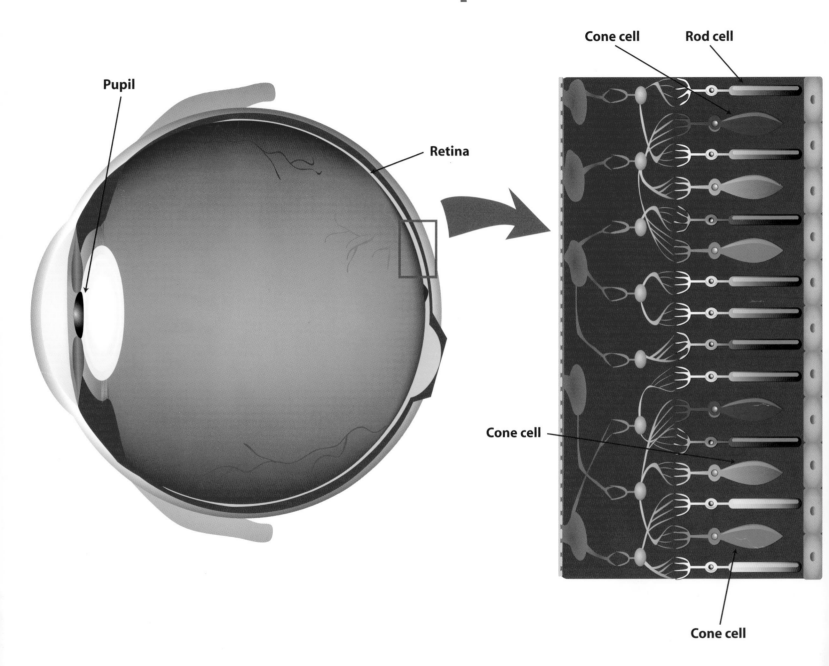

To figure out what was wrong with Corey's eyes, doctors tested his deoxyribonucleic acid (DNA). At six years old, he was diagnosed with the genetic disease Leber congenital amaurosis Type 2, or LCA2.

There was no treatment. Corey was going to go blind.

A Dam in the River

Vision begins when light enters through the pupil of the eye and strikes the retina at the back of the eye. The retina contains two types of light-detecting cells, or photoreceptors: Rods detect brightness, and three types of cones detect color. Together, rods and cones capture visual information and send it to the brain.

Rod cells can detect light because they contain rhodopsin, a pigment made up of protein and a special form of vitamin A. The vitamin A changes shape when light

+ Leber Congenital Amaurosis

Leber congenital amaurosis (LCA) was first described by German ophthalmologist Theodor Leber in 1869. As well as progressive blindness, the disease causes uncontrolled, quivering eye movements called nystagmus.

LCA affects approximately three out of every 100,000 babies worldwide.[3] Defective *RPE65* genes are to blame for up to 16 percent of cases.[4] Seventeen other genes are also involved in LCA. Because functions of the eyes are complicated, many genes are involved in making them work.

Three types of photoreceptor cone cells and one type of photoreceptor rod cell in the human eye convert light into vision signals sent to the brain.

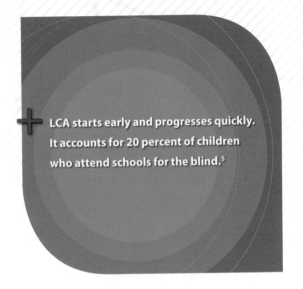

LCA starts early and progresses quickly. It accounts for 20 percent of children who attend schools for the blind.[5]

hits it, creating the visual signal. Before rhodopsin can respond to light again, the vitamin A portion has to be converted back to its original form. In a healthy eye, this is done by an enzyme called retinal pigment epithelium-specific protein 65kDa (RPE65). Patients with LCA2, such as Corey, have weakened or missing *RPE65* enzymes.

The conversion of vitamin A requires a molecular cascade with several intermediate steps, each dependent on the one before. Defective or missing *RPE65* creates a dam that blocks the cascade. The used form of vitamin A builds up behind the dam and is not changed back to its original, light-sensitive form. That means downstream, the light-sensitive form of vitamin A is rare or missing, and so is rhodopsin. In young patients, this blockage impairs vision. Over time, however, the blockage also kills the rod cells, damaging the retina. As a result of this damage, most LCA2 patients are completely blind by the age of 30 or 40.

But what if there were a way to remove the dam, by replacing the *RPE65* enzyme? Could Corey be cured? Doctors Bennett and Albert Maguire of the University of Pennsylvania thought it might be possible.

The Dogs Are Spinning!

In 1988, 12 years before Corey was born, scientist and veterinarian Kristina Narfström was contacted by a Briard sheepdog breeder who was concerned about vision problems in some of her dogs. In a litter of nine puppies, five tested positive for poor vision, especially in dim light.

Narfström discovered the dogs had an error in the gene for *RPE65*—the same faulty gene responsible for LCA2 in humans. That meant Briards would make good models for studying human blindness. They could also be

Clinical Trials

Before a new drug or gene therapy can be tested on people, it must first pass preclinical trials. These trials are done on animals or in petri dishes full of human cells, testing the therapy for safety and effectiveness. However, 80 to 90 percent of new therapies never make it past the preclinical trial stage.[6]

Promising treatments enter Phase 1 clinical trials, which test the safety of new treatments in humans. Corey Haas underwent a Phase 1 clinical trial. There are also Phase 2 and Phase 3 clinical trials. Phase 2 trials test for effectiveness. Phase 3 trials test a large number of patients. A potential therapy must pass every phase before it can be sold to the public.

used to test an experimental treatment called gene therapy. This is a way of treating disease by replacing faulty genes with healthy ones.

Scientists such as Bennett and Maguire expanded upon Narfström's work in the following years. In 2000, the year of Corey's birth, Bennett's research group attempted gene therapy on a trio of blind Briards, including one named Lancelot. Maguire used a tiny needle to insert billions of copies of a healthy *RPE65* gene under Lancelot's right retina. The two other blind Briards received the same treatment, which took just minutes to complete.

Many Briards that have regained their sight through gene therapy have been adopted by families with children who have hereditary blindness.

The team did not expect what happened next. A few days after the surgery, a lab worker checked on the Briards. "The dogs are spinning! They're spinning!" the worker shouted.[7] The dogs had regained vision in their right eyes. And they were turning in circles to see as much of the world as they possibly could.

Corey's Clinical Trial

Seven years after receiving treatment, the three Briards could still see. This lasting success meant it was time to try the *RPE65* gene therapy on people. Three groups of scientists, including Bennett and Maguire's team, launched Phase 1 clinical trials on humans. Each trial included three volunteers with LCA2 who were 17 years old or older.

Vision improved in seven out of nine volunteers.[8] And a trend was apparent in the data: the younger the patient, the better the results. The next step was to test the treatment on

Bennett and Maguire: Gene Therapy Dream Team

Jean Bennett is a physician and molecular geneticist. Her husband, Albert Maguire, is the surgeon who operated on Corey. Bennett and Maguire met in medical school when they were assigned to dissect the same human head.

According to Maguire, he and his wife have found their work on genetic blindness to be very rewarding. "There's a huge emotional overlay," Maguire said. "Doctors have always regarded [these diseases] as incurable and told patients there is nothing we can do for you. The fact that [gene therapy] seems to be working is extremely exciting."[9]

Bennett and Maguire's team was launching a Phase 3 clinical trial for LCA2 in January 2013. Patients were being reunited throughout spring 2013.

children. Scientists hoped if children with LCA2 received the healthy gene before their retinas started to break down, they might never go blind.

Corey was one child who participated in a trial to test this theory. On September 25, 2008, three days after his eighth birthday, Corey arrived at the Children's Hospital of Philadelphia in Pennsylvania for treatment. He was the youngest patient in Bennett and Maguire's trial.

A nurse wrote a red *X* on Corey's forehead to show that his left eye would be treated. While Corey was under anesthesia, tiny metal clips held his left eye open. Maguire cut two holes in Corey's eye. Inserting a light through one hole and a needle through the other, Maguire injected billions of copies of a healthy *RPE65* gene under Corey's retina.

Four days later, Corey's parents took him to the Philadelphia Zoo, where he glanced up at the sky and cried out in terror, "It hurts!"[10] For the first time, the boy who had previously stared at lightbulbs could see the brightness of the sun.

Not a Treatment, But a Cure

After waiting to ensure the left eye had lasting success without complications, Corey's right eye was successfully injected in 2011. The surgeries have had an enormous impact on his life. According to

Corey's father, "His independence has increased, and he's able to play like a normal child now."[11] Today, Corey's vision is almost identical to that of a person without LCA2.

Gene therapy researchers had been working toward a moment like this for decades. Many hereditary diseases were completely untreatable with conventional medicine. The possibility of permanently fixing the genes that caused these diseases was tantalizing. If it worked, scientists could offer much more than treatments—they could offer cures. Human suffering could be reduced as never before.

Cures, however, were much easier to imagine than to achieve. As gene therapy researchers chased their dreams, they encountered enormous scientific challenges, heartbreaking setbacks, and devastating failures. They also faced ethical dilemmas never before encountered in medicine. But after years of struggle and conflict, scientists are finally achieving more successes. Gene therapy is finding its niche, and the possibilities are astonishing.

"One of his friends came over and Corey asked me when she had dyed her hair," Corey's father said after the surgery. "Her hair color hadn't changed. That's when I knew that he was really starting to see colors."[12]

2

Disease and the Double Helix

Since the early days of molecular biology, scientists have fantasized about repairing broken genes. This hope was the driving force behind a long period of trials and failures. Gene therapy treatments being developed today are only possible because of many years of research into basic genetics. It all began in the 1800s, when Austrian monk and botanist Gregor Mendel became the first person to map and measure patterns of heredity.

Mendel looked at pea plants and noticed that certain traits, such as height, varied between individual plants. Using a paintbrush to transfer pollen, he crossbred tall plants with short ones and found 100 percent of the offspring were tall. Mendel determined the tall trait was dominant and the short trait had receded. Next, Mendel bred these offspring with each other and measured the second

A depiction of Gregor Mendel in 1868

Mendel's Crossbred Pea Plants

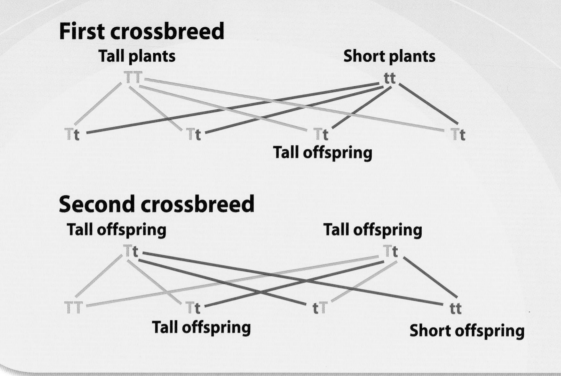

First crossbreed

Tall plants — TT

Short plants — tt

Tt   Tt   Tt   Tt

Tall offspring

Second crossbreed

Tall offspring — Tt

Tall offspring — Tt

TT   Tt   tT   tt

Tall offspring

Short offspring

generation. The pattern changed. Twenty-five percent of the second-generation offspring were short, meaning the recessive short trait had reappeared.

Mendel realized there was only one way to explain these results. Each individual plant had two copies of the "factor" that controlled height, but each parent passed only one copy to its offspring. Offspring that inherited either one or two copies of the dominant tall factor were tall. Plants that

When tall plants breed with short plants, their offspring are all tall, but the second generation can be tall or short.

inherited two copies of the recessive short factor were short. This came to be known as Mendelian inheritance. Mendel published these groundbreaking discoveries in 1865. But their importance would not be recognized for 35 years.

Heredity in Humans

One reason Mendelian inheritance was overlooked was because Mendel did not know what biological process actually controlled the patterns of heredity he described. In 1902, shortly after Mendel's rules were rediscovered, scientists Walter Sutton and Theodor Boveri suggested the factors that control traits might be carried on the chromosomes. Chromosomes are enormous single molecules of DNA that are tightly wrapped around complex substances called proteins. They had previously been observed. In 1909, Mendel's factors were renamed "genes." In the 1920s, "genome," a fusion of the words *gene* and *chromosome*, was coined to describe an individual's total hereditary material.

Selective breeding, as Mendel used in his plant experimentation, is the oldest form of gene manipulation. It began with the domestication of dogs from wolves more than 14,000 years ago.

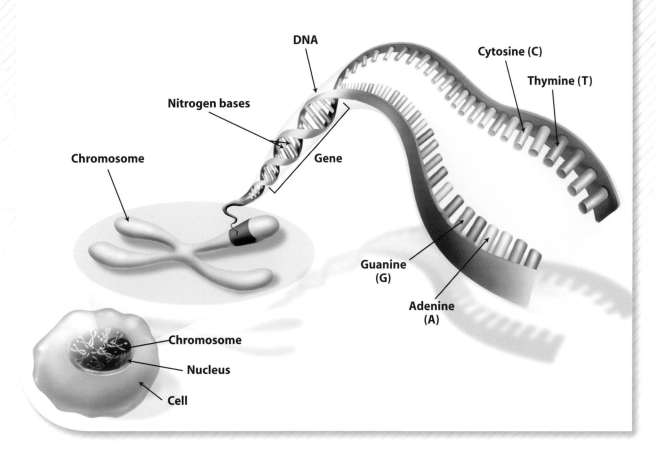

Labels: DNA · Nitrogen bases · Chromosome · Gene · Cytosine (C) · Thymine (T) · Guanine (G) · Adenine (A) · Chromosome · Nucleus · Cell

The Double Helix

It was now clear that DNA carried inheritable instructions for life. But how did DNA pass from cell to cell, and from parent to child? The key was in its shape, which was described by scientists James Watson and Francis Crick in 1953.

The nucleus of each cell contains chromosomes made of wound DNA. Genes are made up of DNA. Each gene consists of many pairs of nitrogen bases.

DNA is a double-stranded helix, often compared to a twisted ladder. Chains of sugar and phosphate molecules make up the ladder's side rails. The rungs are made of pairs of nitrogen bases, forming the chemical bonds that hold the strands together. In DNA, there are four nitrogen bases: adenine (A), cytosine (C), guanine (G), and thymine (T). These bases only pair in two ways: G always bonds with C, and A always bonds with T. DNA makes up several genes within the chromosome. A gene is a specific place in the DNA consisting of a string of nitrogen bases. Genes determine inherited traits.

Bonding between bases is the key to heredity. Body cells divide as a human being grows. When a body cell divides, it produces two daughter cells. Each daughter cell needs a full set of chromosomes. The DNA from the original cell must be replicated to provide this. During replication, an enzyme breaks the bonds between the DNA's bases, separating the strands of the helix. Two new

Discovering DNA's Structure

In 1951, Rosalind Franklin began working with physicist-turned-biologist Maurice Wilkins at King's College in London, England. Franklin studied the shape of DNA using X-ray crystallography, which is a method for analyzing the atomic structure of molecules. In January 1953, Franklin captured an image of DNA that Wilkins showed to scientists James Watson and Francis Crick without her knowledge. Crick said the photo was critical to their discovery of the double helix. But, while Franklin was acknowledged, she received lesser credit. Franklin died of cancer at age 37. Three years later, in 1962, Wilkins, Watson, and Crick were awarded the Nobel Prize for discovering the structure of DNA.

strands are made, each using one old strand as a template. The result is two complete sets of daughter DNA molecules, each set containing one old strand and one new. It takes approximately 15 minutes to copy the entire genome. The newly copied chromosomes are then sorted into the daughter cells.

Until 1956, the normal number of chromosomes in a human cell was thought to be 48. But that year, scientists discovered that the true number is actually 46. There are 22 pairs called autosomes, plus the X and Y sex-determining chromosomes. Females have two X chromosomes, while males have one X and one Y.

Only genes on the autosomes follow Mendel's patterns of inheritance. Y-chromosome genes only affect males. X-chromosome genes affect males and females differently. In the case of X-chromosome diseases, a female's normal, dominant chromosome will mask the effect of a recessive disease gene found on her second X chromosome. She will be a carrier for the disease, but will not suffer its effects.

Laid end to end, the chromosomes in one human cell are less than 0.02 inches (0.5 mm) long. However, if the DNA within were unwound and stretched out, it would be as tall as an average man.[1]

Chromosomes in a human cell: 22 autosomes and the X and Y chromosomes

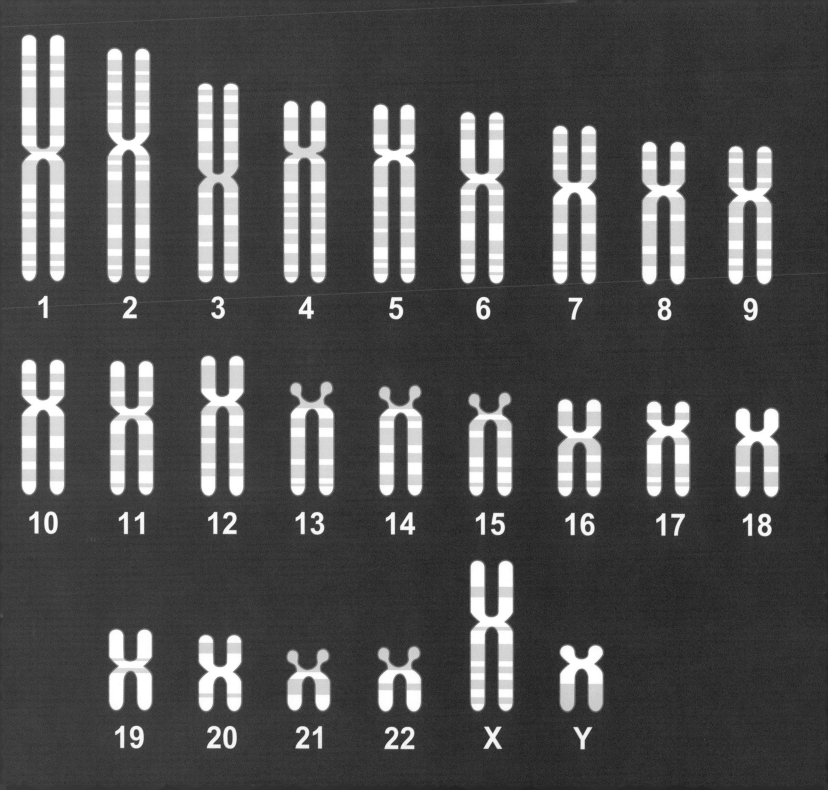

However, males have only one X chromosome, and therefore only one copy of each gene. In males, recessive X-chromosome genes act as dominant traits. If a mother carries an X-chromosome disease, her male children will either get the diseased X-chromosome and be affected, or they will get the healthy X chromosome and be normal.

How Genes Encode Proteins

Proteins are some of the most important molecules in the body. Proteins form nerves and muscles, fight infections, break down foods, and much more. The instructions for making these proteins are in genes.

The genetic code is called "universal" because the codons are the same across almost all species. For example, the bases CCG encode the same amino acid in elephants, eggplants, and even bacteria.

Amino acids are the building blocks of proteins. There are 20 different amino acids in proteins, but just four nitrogen bases in DNA. Specialized enzymes in the cell read the nitrogen bases in groups of three. Each group of three is called a codon. Each codon signifies a specific amino acid. A set of codons contains the genetic information for a complete protein. An amino acid chain is formed from the information in these codons. The chain twists and folds to become a protein.

But protein construction does not occur in the same part of the cell where the instructions are found. Chromosomes, and therefore genes, are protected inside the nucleus. Protein construction occurs outside the nucleus, in the cytoplasm. To make a protein, the gene is transcribed, or copied, from the DNA into a messenger molecule called ribonucleic acid (RNA). The RNA is spliced, or broken, into sub-type messenger RNA (mRNA). This exports, or carries, the instructions from the nucleus to the cytoplasm, where the sequence of codons is translated and folded into a chain of amino acids. This creates a working protein.

DNA and Disease

As Mendel described, different individuals may have different versions of the same gene. These versions are caused by mutations, or changes to the sequence of DNA bases. Depending on the type of change, mutations may have no effect on the protein, may weaken the protein, or may completely destroy the protein's function. Weak and missing proteins sometimes cause genetic disease. In gene therapy, undamaged genes are inserted into a patient so the body reads the correct instructions and produces functional proteins.

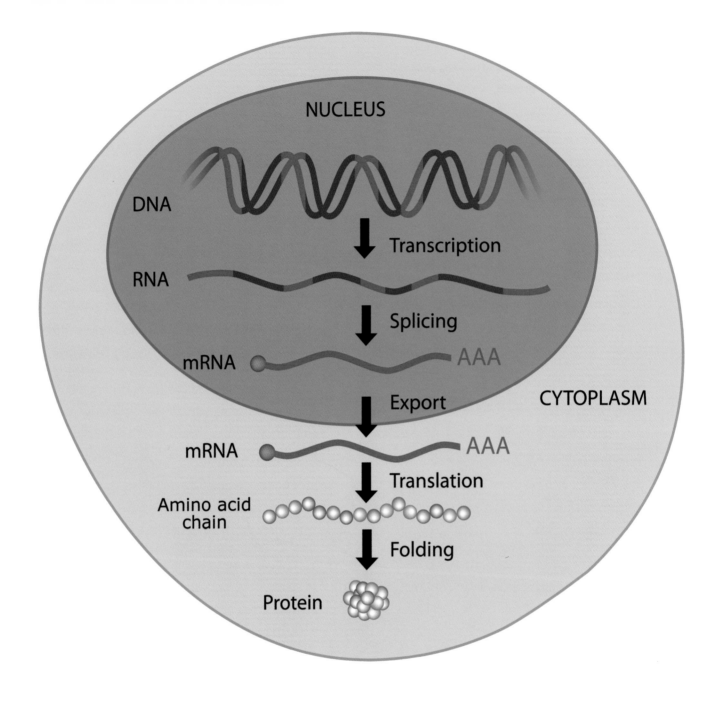

RNA is exported from the nucleus as mRNA and into the cytoplasm, where it is translated into the amino acid chain that becomes a protein.

Before modern gene therapy became possible, three tools were developed. One was the Human Genome Project (HGP), which created a map of all the genes in human DNA. The others were recombinant DNA technology, which merged DNA from two species, and techniques for getting foreign DNA into human cells. The history of all three is filled with controversy.

Beneficial Mutations

Sickle cell anemia was the first disease for which a gene and a mutation were identified. It is an autosomal recessive condition, meaning the disease only develops when two copies of a mutated gene are present. The disease is often fatal to those affected by it. However, carriers of the disease survive mosquito-borne malaria more often than people without the mutation. Because of this benefit, evolution has favored the sickle cell mutation in geographical areas with malaria, including much of Africa. The mutation is so common that the disease affects one in 400 Americans of African descent.[2]

Recombinant DNA

In September 1962, a mother brought her young son to the hospital, complaining of "sand" in his diaper. The sandy substance turned out to be crystals of uric acid, which is a chemical found in bird droppings. This intrigued Doctor William Nyhan, as did the bandages on the boy's hands. When the bandages were unwrapped, Nyhan was horrified to discover the child had bitten off the tips of his own fingers. "The minute I saw him, I knew that this was a [genetic disease], and that somehow all of these things we were seeing were related," Nyhan said.[1]

The disease afflicting the boy became known as Lesch-Nyhan syndrome. It is caused by mutations in an X-chromosome gene called *HPRT*. Because this gene is recessive and gender-linked, the condition affects boys only. Patients feel as much pain as healthy people, but have no control

As William Nyhan's first patient did, many children with Lesch-Nyhan syndrome bite off the tips of their fingers or inflict other self-harm.

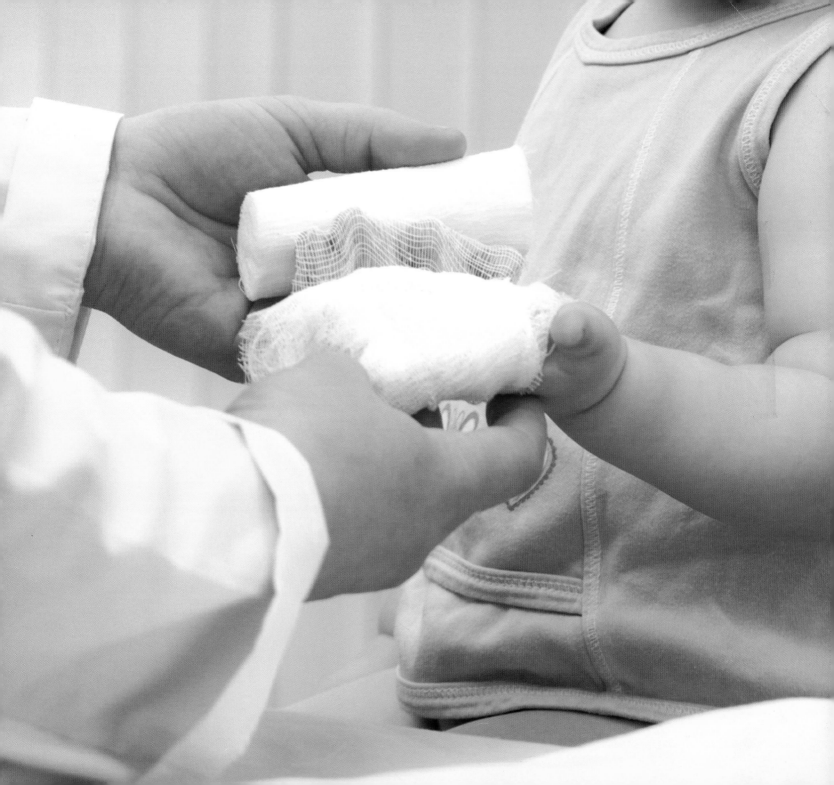

A Destructive Disease

Lesch-Nyhan syndrome affects a few hundred people living in the United States today. While a mutation present in the *HPRT* gene is always responsible, there is no single DNA defect that causes Lesch-Nyhan. Instead, each family carries its own unique mutation. Scientists believe the destructive behaviors that make the disease so shocking are caused by faulty signals between brain cells. They are an extreme expression of the urge most people get to pop zits or chew their fingernails.

over their self-destructive impulses. One boy with the syndrome put his hands inside his mouth and tore out the bones in his own face.

Scientists were desperate to repair the DNA defect causing these shocking symptoms. In the 1960s, some of the first preclinical gene therapy experiments ever conducted were for Lesch-Nyhan. Researchers grew patients' cells in petri dishes and exposed them to pieces of naked DNA, which are pieces of DNA that do not have any association with particular compounds or tissues. They hoped the patients' cells would spontaneously take up the right piece of DNA and begin producing the missing HPRT enzyme. It did not work. One problem was that naked DNA has a hard time getting through a cell's outer membrane. Also, the scientists were using a collection of DNA pieces containing the entire human genome. The chance that the cells would take in the one gene for *HPRT* out of all of those fragments was very slim. If gene therapy was going to work, for Lesch-Nyhan or any other disease, new methods of isolating genes and getting them into cells would have to be developed.

Combining Chromosomes

In 1969, scientists studying bacteria discovered a new type of enzyme. Called restriction enzymes, they defend bacteria against invading viruses. Viruses consist of DNA wrapped in a protein shell. When viruses enter other cells, the host cells are forced to replicate the virus chromosomes, create new shells, and produce new viruses. Restriction enzymes stop this from happening to bacteria cells by cutting the viral DNA into pieces. Each enzyme recognizes a specific sequence of DNA bases and only cuts the DNA where that pattern occurs. This was an important discovery: if scientists knew the sequence of a gene they wanted to experiment with, they could cut out the entire gene just by choosing the right enzyme.

In 1928, scientist Fred Griffith discovered that different bacterial cells could exchange genetic traits. In 1944, researchers realized bacteria did this using their natural ability to exchange DNA. This was the first suggestion that DNA was the hereditary material.

For example, the restriction enzyme *Eco*R1 cuts DNA wherever it finds the sequence GAATTC. In DNA, the strands of the double helix run in opposite directions. Instead of cutting through both strands of DNA in the same physical place on either side of the strand, it breaks each DNA strand between matching base locations: between the G and the A on each side. This creates DNA fragments with "sticky" unpaired bases at either end. These bases look for matching sequences to bond with—and it does not matter which species the DNA comes from. Using restriction enzymes, DNA from any organism could now be joined to DNA from any other organism. These molecules became known as recombinant DNA.

Pure Genes

A second major breakthrough also occurred in 1969. Jonathan Beckwith became the first geneticist to isolate a single gene from an entire genome. The implications of his discovery alarmed him. "The more we think about it," Beckwith said that year, "the more we realize [this method] could be used to purify [and remix] genes in higher organisms. The steps do not exist now, but it is not inconceivable that within not too long, it could be used, and it becomes more and more frightening."[2]

Scientists could now mix and match genes in a test tube. They wondered if they could also insert these new sequences into living things, giving creatures genes they had never had before. Could

Making Recombinant DNA with *EcoR1*

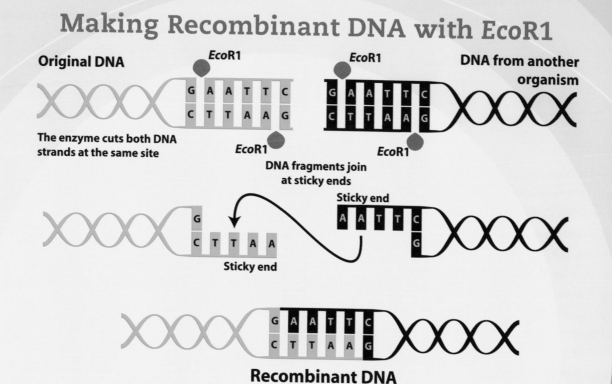

gene therapists now insert specific genes into patients with genetic diseases? More important, they wondered, should they? Scientist Paul Berg was about to answer these questions.

First Attempts

The first gene therapy trial on living patients took place in 1970, before recombinant DNA technology existed. Virologist Stanfield Rogers and his colleagues gave two girls a virus that normally infects rabbits. In rabbits, the virus leads to production of an enzyme that both girls were missing. However, that enzyme is produced from the rabbits' original gene. Since the girls' genes were defective, and the virus did not carry a replacement copy, the experiment was a failure. Because Rogers' team knew so little about the virus and the girls' disease, other scientists condemned this research as reckless and unethical.

Berg's Dilemma

Berg studied DNA, RNA, and protein synthesis, or the production of proteins. In 1970, he became interested in viruses.

Virus behavior—entering and forcing host cells to replicate virus chromosomes and protein shells and produce new viruses—made viruses ideal prototype systems for inserting genes into cells. Using restriction enzymes, Berg thought it would be possible to insert the gene of his choice into the chromosome of a virus. The virus could then deliver that gene into human cells, where the gene would be translated into protein. If the method worked, gene therapy would become a real possibility.

In 1971, Berg designed his recombinant DNA using a virus called SV40 as the vector, or delivery agent. He planned to test it by inserting it into the bacteria *E. coli*,

which live in human intestines, before moving on to mammal cells. However, geneticist Robert Pollack expressed concerns to Berg about the experiment. Pollack thought putting foreign DNA into *E. coli* might create a deadly new superbug.

At first, Berg was skeptical of this possibility. But after thinking it over, he realized he really did not know what might happen. So he stopped his experiment and called a meeting to discuss the risks and

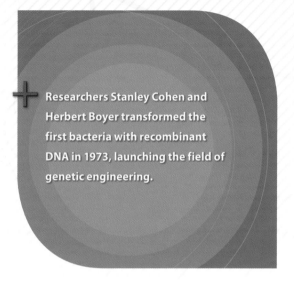

Researchers Stanley Cohen and Herbert Boyer transformed the first bacteria with recombinant DNA in 1973, launching the field of genetic engineering.

ethics of this powerful new technology. "Ninety percent of the guys clapped and slavered about what you would be able to do with [recombinant DNA technology]," Berg says. "Ten percent of the guys said you could also do some nasty things, or some nasty things might occur inadvertently. So the question arose, do we have an obligation to say anything [to the public]?"[3]

The scientists decided they did. In 1974, Berg's group recommended that potentially dangerous recombinant DNA experiments should be postponed until the risk could be studied. As a result, the National Institutes of Health (NIH) established the Recombinant DNA Advisory Committee (RAC), which became responsible for regulating all recombinant DNA research. RAC later joined with the Food and Drug Administration (FDA) to approve all gene therapy trials in humans.

With these protections in place, scientists cautiously continued looking for ways to add new genes to living organisms. "In the end, we gained the public's trust," Berg said. "Scientists were able to look at an issue they had raised and deal with it in a way that people could disagree with, but that by and large had worked. And has worked spectacularly well, because there has been no incident in billions of experiments."[4]

Gene Therapy Becomes Possible

While Berg and colleagues talked about mutant superbugs, other researchers raised the possibility of applying recombinant technology to gene therapy. Going from bacteria to humans would be challenging, though. How could scientists target the correct body part, preventing genes from being expressed in the wrong place? Would patients have allergic reactions to the new proteins? What if inserting a gene into a patient's chromosomes created a new mutation? Years of preclinical research would be needed before gene therapy could be safely tested on humans in clinical trials.

Cloning Genes

Paul Berg said that when most people hear the word "cloning," they automatically think "copies of people." When scientists use the word, they usually mean something totally different: using living organisms as "photocopiers" for recombinant DNA. "We take a virus, and we [use bacteria to] make a million copies, and we've cloned the virus," explained Berg.[5] This technique is used to create millions of copies of DNA sequences for research or gene therapy.

In 1978, researchers Werner Arber, Daniel Nathans, and Hamilton Smith won a Nobel Prize for discovering restriction enzymes. Two years later, Paul Berg also won a Nobel Prize for his pioneering work on recombinant DNA.

However, in 1980, scientist Martin Cline conducted the first recombinant DNA gene therapy trial on humans in defiance of the RAC, which had rejected his research. Cline's trial failed, and because he had violated ethical and legal standards for human experimentation, his career was destroyed.

It was not until 1984 that Doctor Theodore Friedmann's team succeeded in giving a working *HPRT* gene to cells isolated from Lesch-Nyhan patients. According to Friedmann, it was the first experiment using recombinant DNA technology to demonstrate that a defect could be corrected by adding a gene. The same year, Friedmann's team proved that the human gene could be used to transform cells in living mice.

But now the question became how to go from preclinical studies to the complex work of correcting the syndrome in humans. "It's like an onion," Friedmann said. "The more we peel away, the more we

want to cry because it's so complicated."[6] Despite continued research, an effective gene therapy for Lesch-Nyhan had not been found as of 2013.

The Human Genome Project: Hunting Genes

In the 1960s, 1970s, and 1980s, some geneticists were so enchanted by the dream of "fixing" the human genome and eliminating genetic disease forever that they made some questionable decisions. These scientists included virologist Stanfield Rogers, who conducted a failed trial in 1970, knowing so little about what he was doing that his actions were deemed reckless. Ten years later came Cline's defiant, failed attempt to conduct the first recombinant DNA gene therapy trial on humans.

Recombinant DNA technology improved in the 1980s and made it possible to insert replacement DNA into living things. But gene therapy would not work unless scientists knew which piece of DNA needed replacing. Disease genes had to be identified first.

The human genome of 46 chromosomes, with bands representing genes

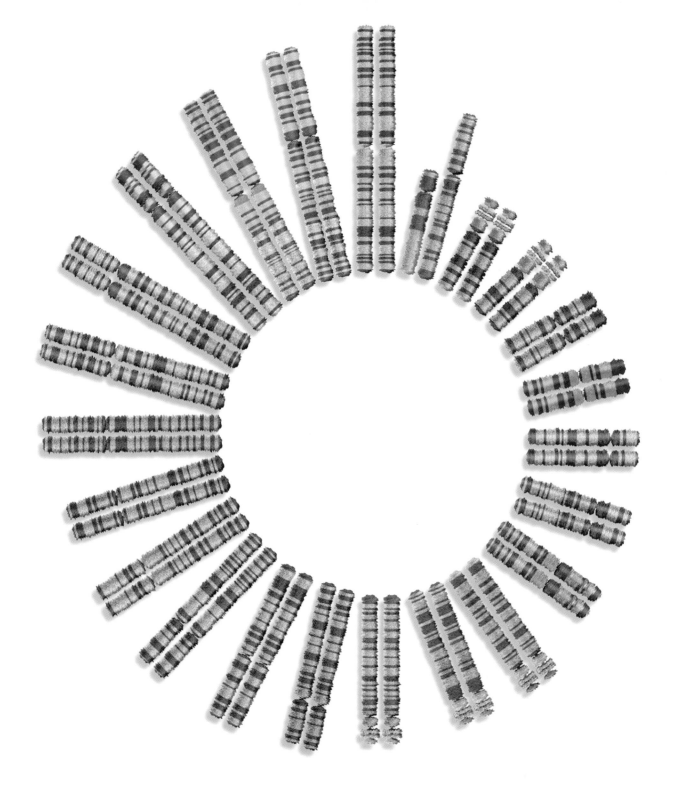

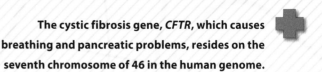

Cystic fibrosis is one of the most common Mendelian diseases in people with European ancestors. In the United States alone, millions of people carry cystic fibrosis. These carriers are healthy but contain one copy of the recessive mutation, which can be passed on to offspring.

Thirty thousand people in the United States have cystic fibrosis.[1] The disease causes sticky mucus to build up in a patient's lungs. Bacteria get trapped in the mucus, leading to infections and eventual death. Even with antibiotics and physical therapy, patients usually die by the age of 30.

In 1981, scientists began hunting for the cystic fibrosis gene. By 1985, they knew it was somewhere on human chromosome number seven. To close in on the right spot, scientists looked for DNA sequences that cystic fibrosis patients had in common. Finally, in 1989, geneticist Francis Collins and his research team identified the correct gene sequence.

Later, Collins recalled the frustrations of the eight-year search. "That experience convinced me that . . . we had to have a much more systematic way of doing things," he said.[2] One author described the process of looking for genes as trying to "parachute into the dark continent of the genome hoping to find a mountaintop."[3] Researchers decided they would have more success if they had a map. In May 1985, researcher Robert Sinsheimer proposed the creation of such a map, by sequencing the entire human genome.

Cystic Fibrosis

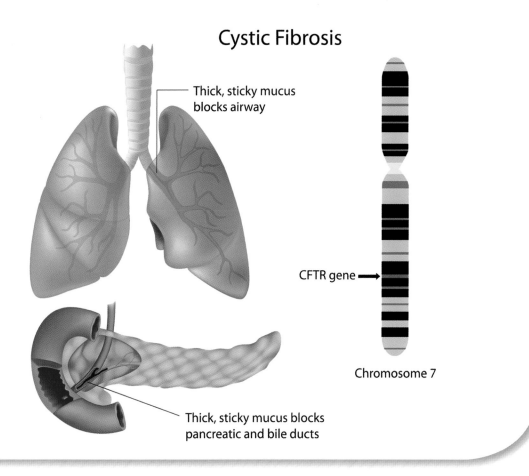

Thick, sticky mucus blocks airway

CFTR gene

Chromosome 7

Thick, sticky mucus blocks pancreatic and bile ducts

Scientists and government agencies immediately began arguing over the cost and value of such a project. But by May 1987, Watson, the scientist who had first described the double helix, began visiting the US Congress to try to raise funds for the project. In 1990, the NIH launched the Human Genome Project (HGP). Its goal was to determine the order of all 3 billion base pairs in one human's DNA, down

Amplifying and Sequencing

Invented in 1983, the polymerase chain reaction (PCR) is DNA replication in a test tube. PCR is used to make millions of copies of DNA for research and law enforcement. Crime labs use PCR to amplify DNA from tiny forensic samples, in order to create a DNA profile that is unique to an individual of interest.

The DNA sequencing methods of the HGP are also a type of PCR. Instead of replicating the whole gene, sequencing uses special "terminator" nitrogen bases to produce a set of DNA fragments. Each one of these fragments is one base longer than the next. The terminator bases incorporated at the end of each fragment are labeled with fluorescent tags, allowing scientists to identify them.

to the last G, A, T, and C. The data could then be used to locate genes and figure out which mutations caused which diseases.

Determining the genome sequence would be extremely complicated and very expensive. In 1990, it cost more than ten dollars to identify a single DNA base.[4] The work was also time-consuming. An experienced scientist could only sequence between 50 and 100 bases per day. Soon robots and computers were developed to do the work, which made the process faster and less costly. But a new problem was brewing: a fight between scientists working on the HGP.

Craig Venter v. the NIH

Biologist Craig Venter began working for the NIH in 1984. By 1991, Venter had identified hundreds of gene fragments. He wanted the NIH to patent them, giving the organization control over any research and drug development based on those genes. As leader of the HGP, Watson was against patenting; he believed DNA sequences should be free and publicly available. To Watson's dismay, however, higher powers at the NIH agreed with Venter and supported Venter's application for the patent. Watson quit the project in 1992. And although the patent office turned down the application, private companies went on to file successful patents in later years.

Collins took over running the HGP. Consistent with policies Watson had established, his researchers used careful, deliberate techniques to isolate DNA sequences from each chromosome. Their data was very accurate, but despite technological improvements, the method still was relatively slow. Venter believed something called shotgun sequencing would be much quicker. This method involves breaking the entire genome into small, random pieces. Each piece is sequenced, and supercomputers then look for overlapping areas, putting the pieces back together.

Patenting Life

As of June 18, 2012, 63,368 DNA-based patents had been issued.[5] DNA patents give owners the sole right to develop therapies that target the gene for 17 years. The patents allow drug companies to control sale of their products, making back the money they spent on research. If other researchers want to study a patented gene, they have to pay a licensing fee to the patent holder. Profit is often a strong motivator for research. According to Venter, "If you have a disease, you'd better hope someone patents the gene for it."[6] The flip side is that patenting prevents other researchers from working with the gene, potentially slowing down research.

Shotgun sequencing had been used for the single chromosomes of microorganisms. Venter wanted to apply it to the complex human genome. Collins and his team felt this method was too messy and unreliable. As a result of conflicts concerning his ideas about shotgun sequencing, Venter also quit the NIH in 1992.

On May 8, 1998, Venter met with Collins, who was still leading the HGP. Venter announced that his new for-profit company, Celera Genomics, was going to shotgun sequence the entire human genome. Furthermore, Venter claimed he would do this for less money and be finished four years before the projected end date for NIH's HGP. Collins's team believed Venter was trying to steal credit for sequencing the genome and profit by selling the data.[7] Venter denied he wanted to profit from the genome, citing scientific curiosity as his motive. Venter further angered the NIH scientists on May 12, 1998, when he told reporters the NIH scientists should start sequencing the DNA of mice instead.

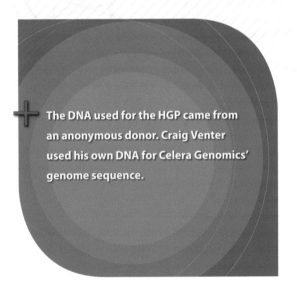

The DNA used for the HGP came from an anonymous donor. Craig Venter used his own DNA for Celera Genomics' genome sequence.

After several years of conflict, scientists on both sides reached a compromise. On June 26, 2000, Collins and Venter appeared together at the White House. The two shared their data and revealed a first draft of the human genome sequence that night. Today, the data from the HGP is freely available in the online database GenBank. Celera Genomics' data has not been made public, although much of it was incorporated into the publicly available database.

The Book of Life

Before the sequencing of an entire human genome was completed, scientists believed humans had between 50,000 and 140,000 genes. But the HGP revealed there are only approximately 20,500—good news for researchers hunting for genes that cause disease.[8] By 2010, just seven years after the HGP was completed, researchers had discovered the genetic basis of approximately 2,700 diseases.[9]

"A decade from now, once researchers have identified all human genes and their variants, finding a mutation that causes a specific disease will be as easy as typing a book title into Amazon.com."

—*Geneticist Ricki Lewis, 2012*[13]

It had taken 13 years and $2.6 billion dollars for the HGP to sequence the complete genome of one human being.[10] Since the HGP began, technology improved so much that another research group, the 1000 Genomes Project, was able to sequence 1,092 complete human genomes in five years.[11] They completed the work between 2007 and 2012 for only $120 million.[12] The 1000 Genomes Project has plans to sequence an additional 1,500 genomes over the next few years. Their goal is to identify which bases out of the 3 billion differ from human to human, aiding the search for genes. As it turns out, approximately 10 percent of the sequence varies. Of these variable sites, which are spread throughout the genome, up to 20 variants may be recessive mutations that could cause genetic disease in a person's offspring.[14]

Collins has no doubt that this kind of sequence information is valuable for science and medicine. He said the human genome is "a transformative textbook of medicine, with insights that will give health care providers immense new powers to treat, prevent and cure disease."[15]

This is assuming, however, that gene therapy researchers can get replacement genes into living patients. Unfortunately, early attempts to harness viruses for human gene therapy have had unexpected and heartbreaking consequences.

Model Species

The genomes of several model, or nonhuman, species also were sequenced as part of the HGP. This is because many of the genes found in humans also occur in simpler species, which can be used for preclinical research. Nematode worms and insects are two examples. Worms revealed how embryos develop into fully formed creatures. Fruit flies are great for studying the inheritance of Mendelian genes because they reproduce quickly and because there is a long tradition of fruit fly genetic research on which scientists can draw for information.

Mammals are also useful for genetic research, especially mice and dogs. This is because researchers are able to genetically alter mice to create models for human disease. And many dog breeds already have genetic diseases, such as LCA2, that are also found in humans.

5

Fever Dreams and Rude Awakenings

Before and during the HGP, gene therapy researchers were convinced their work was about to launch a medical revolution. Geneticist W. French Anderson was one of the most passionate and outspoken of the scientists working at this time. Unlike some of his predecessors, Anderson was determined to design gene therapy treatments based both on good science and on good ethics.

Anderson and Ashi

A patient in one of Anderson's trials, Ashanti DeSilva, known as Ashi, got her first infection when she was two days old, and they just kept coming. Ashi's parents had to keep her at home to avoid exposing her to germs. In 1988, at two years old, Ashi was diagnosed with severe combined

Gene therapy pioneer W. French Anderson examining gene sequences in a lab

+ Bubble Boy

SCID is sometimes called "bubble boy" disease, after David Phillip Vetter. David was born in 1971 with a version of SCID that affects the X chromosome, called SCID-X1. He lived inside a sterile bubble that protected him from germs. Depressed by his isolated life, David insisted doctors try a bone marrow transplant in hopes that donor tissue would replace his defective cells. On October 21, 1983, David was given some of his sister Katherine's bone marrow. But it turned out Katherine had a normally harmless virus that David's crippled immune system could not fight off. David developed cancer following the treatment, and he died on February 22, 1984.

immunodeficiency disorder (SCID), caused by a mutation in her *ADA* genes. This specific type of the disease is called ADA-SCID.

With ADA-SCID, uric acid builds up in patients' blood, killing the white blood cells that normally kill germs. There were two possible treatments available for Ashi. One was a bone marrow transplant, but doctors could not find a suitable donor. The other, called PEG-ADA, replaced the missing *ADA* in her blood via injections with tiny plastic spheres (called PolyEthylene Glycol) coated in *ADA* enzyme drawn from cows. PEG-ADA treatment costs approximately $250,000 a year.[1] It also gradually stops working in most patients. Unless a third option could be found to treat Ashi, her infections were going to kill her.

The *ADA* gene had been cloned in 1983. ADA-SCID was an ideal test case for gene therapy because the disease was deadly, it was caused by a single gene, and even a small percentage of normal *ADA* production would be enough to allow the immune system to function. Anderson's team planned to use a viral vector to give patients a recombinant *ADA* gene. Viral vectors are viruses that are modified to introduce genetic material into cells. The virus was engineered so its disease-causing genes were removed and replaced with the *ADA* gene, creating a medical delivery vehicle. The virus was supposed to insert the new gene into patients' chromosomes so their blood cells would start making their own *ADA*. Anderson believed Ashi was the perfect candidate for this first approved test of modern gene therapy.

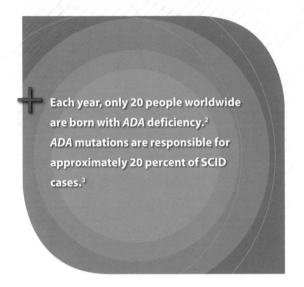

Each year, only 20 people worldwide are born with *ADA* deficiency.[2] *ADA* mutations are responsible for approximately 20 percent of SCID cases.[3]

On September 2, 1990, four-year-old Ashi arrived at the NIH Clinical Center in Bethesda, Maryland. Researchers took a sample of her blood, added the vector, and spent 12 days growing her white blood cells in petri dishes. On September 14, they put billions of Ashi's own cells back into her body. The injection took 28 minutes.

Inside and Out

There are two ways of inserting replacement DNA into patients' cells. Gene therapy for SCID uses the *ex vivo* method, meaning outside the body. Cells are removed from the patient's body, transformed with a vector containing genetic material, cultured, and put back. The *in vivo* method is used for cells and organs that, unlike blood cells, cannot be safely removed. The vector containing the genetic material is injected directly into the patients using *in vivo*, making it harder to control how their bodies react. Deciding which method to use is just one of the questions that makes gene therapy more complicated than other treatments.

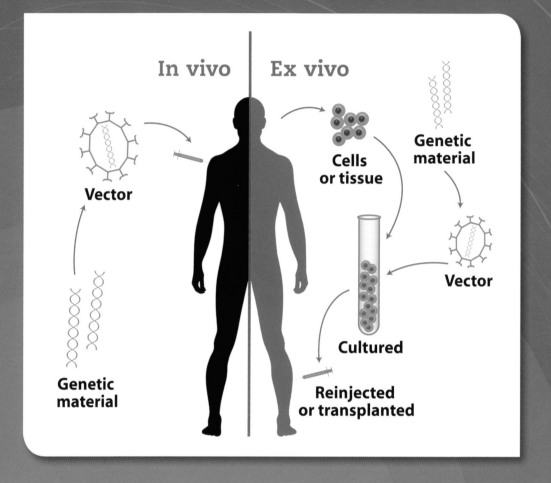

In vivo | Ex vivo

Vector

Genetic material

Cells or tissue

Genetic material

Vector

Cultured

Reinjected or transplanted

Ashi got ten additional injections of cells over the next two years. Eighteen months after the last treatment, her ADA protein levels had increased to one-fourth those of a person without the disease.

Six-year-old Ashanti DeSilva in school in 1993

This was a big enough improvement that her white blood cells were able to survive. Ashi soon enrolled in public kindergarten and was still healthy as of an update released in 2010.

In a 2009 gene therapy trial for ADA-SCID, eight out of ten patients developed healthy immune systems without taking PEG-ADA.[6]

Anderson became known as "the father of gene therapy" after Ashi's successful treatment.[4] But to this day, it is not clear how much of Ashi's recovery was caused by the gene treatment. This is because she never stopped taking PEG-ADA. Anderson's team had felt it was wrong to stop Ashi's PEG-ADA treatments during her gene therapy because it was already known PEG-ADA would help, and no one knew whether gene therapy would. This made sense from an ethical perspective, but also made it impossible to separate the effect of gene therapy from that of the PEG-ADA.

Following Ashi's treatment, clinical gene therapy trials were launched worldwide but with little obvious success. Looking back on those early days, Anderson said, "There was initially a great enthusiasm that lasted three, four years where a couple of hundred trials got started all over the world. Then we came to realize that nothing was really working at the clinical level."[5] Things only got worse from there.

The Worst That Can Happen

On September 17, 1999, 18-year-old Jesse Gelsinger became the first person to die from gene therapy. Gelsinger had an X-chromosome disease called ornithine transcarbamylase deficiency (OTCD) caused by defective *OTC* enzymes. Patients with *OTC* gene mutations cannot break down proteins properly. This causes ammonia—the chemical in window cleaner—to build up in their bodies. If the *OTC* enzymes are missing, boys go into a coma within three days after birth. Half of them die within a month.[7] Gelsinger's enzymes were only weakened, causing a milder form of the disease. Still, he had to eat a strict, low-protein diet and take more than 30 pills every day.

In June 1999, Gelsinger joined a Phase 1 gene therapy clinical trial for OTCD, spearheaded by Doctor James Wilson of the University of Pennsylvania. The trial's goal was to find the maximum safe dose of the viral vector, although researchers hoped patients would get healthier, too. Even a small increase in patients' *OTC* enzymes could have a big effect.

Gelsinger was the second patient to receive the highest dose of vector in the study. On the morning of September 13, 1999, researchers injected the virus into his liver, where the *OTC* enzyme normally works. By that evening, Gelsinger felt feverish. Then his organs started shutting down: liver, lungs, kidneys, and brain. Gelsinger was put on life support. At 2:30 p.m. on September 17, with his doctors and

family gathered around him, Gelsinger's life support systems were unplugged. He died 98 hours after receiving the gene therapy.

Gelsinger's autopsy showed his immune system had tried so hard to kill the vector, it had attacked his own body. Wilson said researchers had spent a decade before the trial trying to engineer a virus that would not have that effect. But it had not been enough to save Gelsinger. Wilson remained confused as to why Gelsinger was the only test subject to react so strongly. He guessed Gelsinger might have been previously infected with the same type of virus as the vector, causing his immune system to recognize a former attacker.

Gelsinger had joined the trial knowing the risks. While he had not needed gene therapy to survive, he wanted to help other patients. Unfortunately, although other patients in the trial survived, their OTCD did not get better. The trial was a failure.

Gelsinger's death was "the end of innocence for gene therapy researchers," according to Collins.[8] Geneticist Leon Rosenberg agreed. "Those were the terrible days," he recalled. "The field bottomed out. The integrity of

Doing It Right

Jesse Gelsinger's trial was about safety, not health benefits. But his father Paul said the scientists misled them by talking about gene therapy as if it were a potential cure for his son. Despite this, during the investigation into Gelsinger's death, Paul said, "These guys screwed up, yes. But they should not be put out of business. . . . I don't want to see anybody suffer like we've suffered. I want them to make this thing work and do it right."[9]

Two-year-old Wilco Conradi interacts with an infant suffering from SCID-XI in 2002. Wilco spent his early life in a bubble as well, before Alain Fischer's gene therapy cured him and gave him a normal life.

science was damaged tremendously."[10] Before the gene therapy research field could recover, tragedy struck again.

Gene Therapy Causes Cancer

Following the blow of Gelsinger's death, gene therapy research limped forward. In 1999, Doctor Alain Fischer of Paris, France, started a gene therapy trial for SCID, the disease Ashi was treated for in the early 1990s. Fischer's focus was a type of SCID caused by damage to the X chromosome, known as SCID-X1. The first two boys treated improved significantly. Therefore, the study was expanded. But things took a terrible turn in 2002 when one of the boys in the trial developed leukemia, a cancer of the blood.

A second boy being treated developed cancer, and the trial was cancelled on January 17, 2003. However, it restarted in May 2004 due to pressure from parents desperate to give their sons a normal life. Out of 20 boys who received the gene therapy, five developed cancer, and one boy died from the cancer.[11] Researchers tried to understand what was happening.

The human genome contains a number of genes that control the timing and speed of cell division. Loss of that control leads to cancer. Fischer's team discovered their viral vector was inserting the replacement SCID-X1 DNA right into what is often called a tumor suppressor gene—one that normally

checks cell division. This caused a new mutation and the boys' leukemia. Avoiding the risk of cancer became a major issue in designing new gene therapies.

Today, 18 of the 20 boys in Fischer's trial are alive, with leukemia being the confirmed cause of only one of those deaths. Of the 18 alive, 17 have working immune systems.[12] Some researchers have argued the risk of death from this gene therapy was much less than the risk of death from bone marrow transplants. However, this case and Gelsinger's proved that gene therapy would only be safe if researchers could find less dangerous vectors.

New Vectors

To make gene therapy safer, scientists needed to find new vectors—ones that did not irritate the immune system or create cancer-causing mutations in the patient's DNA. A family of viruses called adeno-associated viruses (AAVs) seemed to have great potential.

Most people have been naturally infected with an AAV. But these viruses do not cause disease, meaning the immune system has no reason to attack them. Therefore, using AAVs as vectors means deaths such as Gelsinger's should never occur.

AAVs have other advantages that make them useful vectors. The natural forms of these viruses have a gene for a protein called Rep. The Rep protein causes AAVs to insert their DNA at a specific spot on chromosome 19. This is important, as this insertion location is not related to cancer. Scientists are

An illustration depicting the structure of an adeno-associated virus (AAV) used for gene therapy

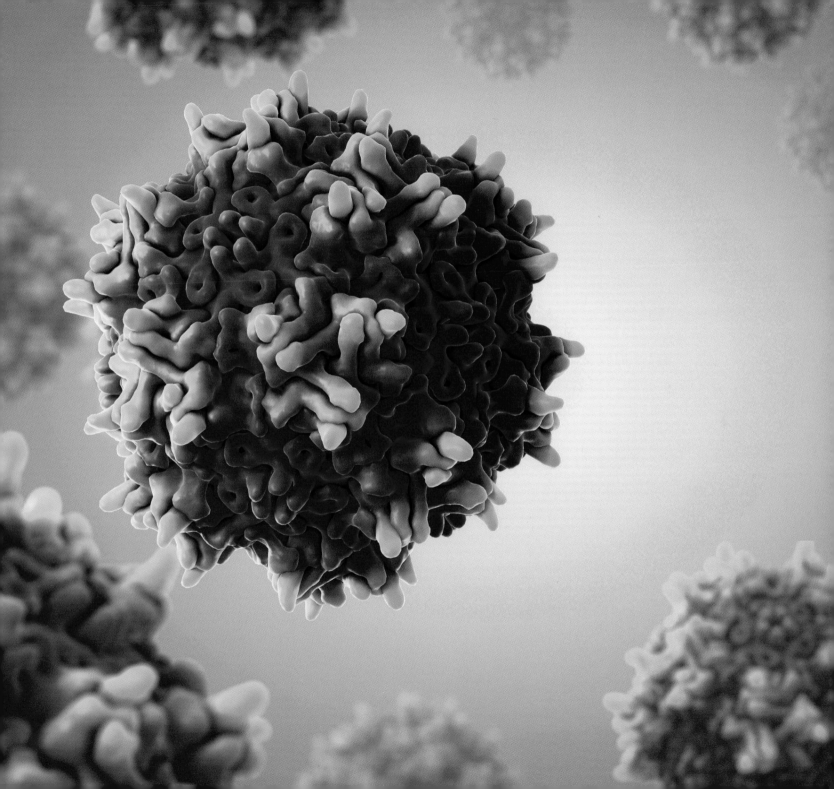

now creating designer vectors that combine the *Rep* gene with the characteristics of other viruses, such as the ability to infect specific organs or carry larger pieces of human DNA.

Scientists also discovered that taking the *Rep* gene out of AAVs destroys their ability to insert themselves into chromosomes. Instead, these recombinant vectors float freely inside the cell. As a result, the therapeutic DNA does not get copied with the patient's chromosomes or reliably passed to daughter cells. This would be a disadvantage for most cell types, which divide regularly and would eventually lose the replacement gene. But some cell types, such as brain and retina, do not divide. In these tissues, floating vectors remain in the cells without creating cancer-causing mutations. For these reasons, Bennett and Maguire chose an AAV vector when restoring Corey's sight.

Healing with HIV

Human immunodeficiency virus (HIV) causes acquired immune deficiency syndrome (AIDS). Because AIDS is contagious and life-threatening, scientists have studied it intensively, allowing them to understand its activity well. This work has allowed

In 2003, Doctor Carl June's research team began the first trial using HIV as a gene therapy vector. The trial was for the treatment of HIV, and four of five patients improved.[1]

them to remove HIV's dangerous genes, turning the virus into a safe and powerful vector. As Wilson said,

> *"It was what everyone had dreamed of. It worked on so many cell lineages, it would open the door to any disease. Of course there was the fear that the public would think we were giving people HIV, but the virus is disabled front, left, and center. It is impossible [for it] to generate [AIDS]."[2]*

Scientists are researching ways to help the HIV vector recognize specific types of human cells, making gene therapy more specific. Cells in different organs can be described as having uniquely shaped locks on their surfaces. By changing the proteins surrounding the vector, scientists can give HIV exactly the right key for these locks, helping ensure new genes only enter the cells where they are needed. For added control, scientists insert

+ Protecting the Brain

Adrenoleukodystrophy (ALD) is an X-chromosome disease that starts destroying affected boys' brains around the age of six years old. Most die before becoming teenagers. Gene therapy trials for ALD began in Paris in 2006. Using an HIV vector and the same ex vivo method that helped the SCID kids, replacement genes were given to four boys between the ages of 3.5 and 7.5 years old. After treatment, two patients improved. Only 10 percent of one boy's cells and 15 percent of another boy's cells contained the healthy ALD protein, but that was enough to prevent further brain damage.[3]

An example of how a virus, such as HIV, carries a therapeutic gene into a cell during gene therapy:

1. The therapeutic gene is inserted into the disabled virus DNA, becoming a vector.

2. The vector enters the cells being treated.

3. The vector breaks down inside the cell, releasing the therapeutic gene and disabled virus DNA into the nucleus.

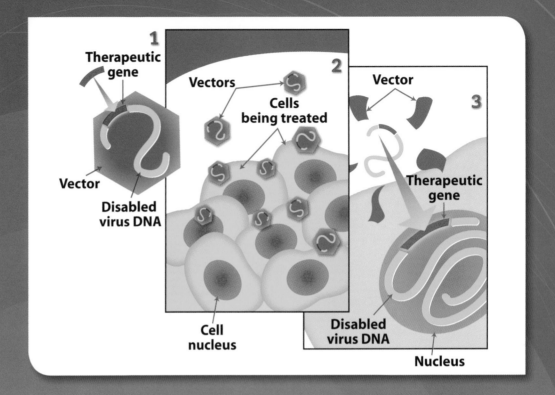

cell-specific on/off switches in the vector DNA. This ensures that replacement genes can only make proteins in the proper tissues.

HIV vectors have a downside, however. Similar to many viruses, HIV inserts its DNA into human chromosomes within the nucleus. This insertion often takes place within a human gene in the chromosome, which increases the risk of mutations. Scientists are researching ways to control this process, but it is challenging. So far, the risk of developing cancer from HIV vectors seems to be low.

Treatments Using Fat Molecules

Viral vectors are getting safer through research, but they still have other disadvantages. For one thing, each virus has a maximum capacity. This means longer human genes will not fit. It is also very expensive to make enough vector viruses for gene therapy treatments. For these reasons, many researchers are developing gene-delivery methods that do not have the drawbacks of these biological vectors.

One such method uses liposomes, which are chemical vectors made of pieces of DNA coated in fat molecules. Liposomes are cheap to make, and the human immune system ignores them. There is also no limit to the amount of DNA they can hold. Unlike viruses, which inject DNA into cells like tiny needles, liposome vectors either fuse with cells or are swallowed whole. Under the right conditions, liposomes are even better at delivering DNA than HIV virus vectors.

In the 1990s, liposomes were used in gene therapy trials for Canavan's disease. Canavan's disease can affect anyone, but it is most common in babies with Jewish ancestry. Starting at birth, these babies' brains develop tiny holes that make them look similar to sponges. These holes cause severe mental and physical disabilities, as well as seizures. Canavan's disease is so devastating some parents have confessed to letting their children die during seizures, rather than condemning them to continued life with the disease.[4]

In 2003, two-year-old Lana Swancey, here with her parents and neuroscientist, was the youngest Canavan's patient ever treated with gene therapy.

Costs and Benefits

Gene therapy research is expensive, and few drug companies want to pay for it. The liposome trial for Canavan's disease was only made possible because the patients' families raised the money. Patient Jacob Sontag's family alone donated more than $200,000 to support the research. [6] "I know in my heart that the gene therapy has kept [Jacob] from slipping into a vegetative state," his mother, Jordana, said years after his treatment. "He is with us, he engages us, he laughs appropriately at what is funny and responds appropriately when we talk to him."[7] The families of other Canavan's gene therapy patients agree the struggle was worth it.

When the first gene therapy trial for the disease began, the only way to get liposomes into Canavan's patients' brains was to drill a 0.35-inch (9 mm) hole into their heads. Then doctors inserted an egg-shaped container under the skin that had a tube running to the brain. Liposomes were added to the container. One of the 16 children in the trial developed a serious brain infection from the treatment.[5] And many of the patients did not improve, likely because the liposome vectors of the time, although safer than viruses, were not very good at entering human cells.

Since the Canavan's trial, scientists have made big improvements to liposome vectors. Changing their shape has helped them better invade cells, and scientists are working on matching the vectors to specific cell types.

For diseases outside of the brain, liposomes can be injected into the blood, which safely and simply carries

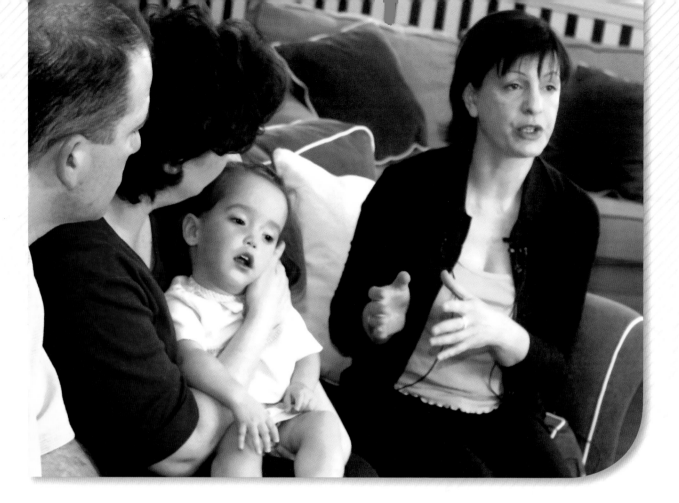

them around the body. This newer method was used in a 2012 Phase 1 clinical trial for patients with incurable lung cancer. Thirty-one patients were given cancer-specific liposomes carrying a gene that slows down cell division in tumors and received a new injection every 21 days. Before gene therapy, every patient's tumors were actively growing. Afterward, five patients' tumors stopped growing for as long as 11 months. In two patients, the tumors shrank.[8] The treatment had few side effects, meaning liposomes will likely be used in many more trials in the future.

Electroshocks and Naked DNA

Scientists learned early in gene therapy research that naked DNA was not very good at getting into human cells. But chances improve when the cells are given electric shocks. Recently, Doctor Jason Dyck and his coworkers at the University of Alberta in Canada used this type of gene therapy to prevent obesity in mice.

Plasmids are small circular chromosomes that bacteria use to exchange antibiotic resistance genes. They are separate from the main bacterial genome.

The treatment used adiponectin, a protein that is rare in obesity patients. Dyck's team added the adiponectin gene to a circular-shaped DNA vector called a plasmid. They sedated the mice and injected the plasmid into the mice's muscles using a needle. Needle electrodes were then used to pass electricity through the muscle before the mice woke up. The electric shocks emitted were very mild and extremely short. They created tiny holes in each mouse's cell membranes, allowing plasmids to enter, and without causing any lasting damage.

After treating the mice, Dyck's team gave them food that was much higher in fat than what they normally ate: 44.9 percent fat, compared to 6.5 percent fat in normal mouse food. After five weeks, the adiponectin mice weighed significantly less than mice that ate high-fat food without receiving gene therapy.[9]

Similar to the viruses used for gene therapy in the 1990s, these newer methods of gene transfer all have disadvantages. But the availability of a range of vectors helps researchers minimize the risks for their patients. It allows them to choose the safest, most effective delivery vehicle for gene therapy.

Inventing the Gene Gun

Instead of using biological or chemical vectors for getting DNA into cells, some scientists are studying the use of physical vectors, called gene guns. In this method, microscopic gold particles coated with healthy DNA are blasted into cells like bullets. The treatment is pain-free and causes no lasting damage. For some types of cells, gene guns work even better than viruses. They are especially useful when genes need to be added to the skin.

From Unicorns to Horses

The failures and setbacks of gene therapy trials in the 1990s were a rude awakening for researchers. Before gene therapy could find its niche, scientists needed to improve the safety of their methods. They also needed to become more realistic about gene therapy's true potential. Gene therapy was not a magic bullet that would instantly and completely eliminate human disease. But properly and cautiously applied, gene therapy could help a lot of people, especially if the techniques could be extended to common, complex conditions.

Many doctors use the saying, "When you hear hoofbeats, think horses, not zebras."[1] This means always start by considering the most common causes of a patient's symptoms. Medical genetics, however, is about the rare and unusual. Giant axonal neuropathy, for example, is a Mendelian disease

Twin brothers with xeroderma pigmentosum must wear suits protecting them from ultraviolet light. Their rare genetic disease is a candidate for gene therapy.

Rare Diseases

According to the National Organization for Rare Diseases (NORD), a rare condition is one that affects fewer than 200,000 people in the United States.[3] When all rare conditions are considered together, however, they add up to more than 25 million Americans altogether.[4] Approximately 200 of these conditions have treatments.[5] That is partly because approximately $1 billion is spent on research before a new therapy is ready to be sold.[6] A rare disease may not affect enough patients for drug companies to make that $1 billion back in drug sales.

In 2009, the NIH launched the Therapeutics for Rare and Neglected Diseases program to fund research for neglected diseases. On July 9, 2012, President Barack Obama signed the FDA Safety and Innovation Act, administering $6 billion to speed up drug approval processes. One focus of the act is rare diseases. Peter L. Saltonstall, president of NORD, was involved in developing this legislation. He said, "Treatments are desperately needed because most [of these diseases] are serious, many are life-threatening, and about two-thirds of the patients are children."[7]

that affects walking, nerve sensation, reflexes, and much more. It affects only 54 people in the entire world.[2] Geneticist Lewis said rare diseases such as this one are the unicorns among the zebras.

Gene therapy research on rare diseases is also paving the way for treatments for common conditions, which is more profitable for drug companies. That is because many rare diseases share characteristics with common ones. The rare condition LCA2, for example, affects the retina. So does macular degeneration, the most common cause of blindness in the western world. Therapy for the rare Canavan's disease requires techniques for getting genes into the brain. These methods could also be used to treat relatively common diseases such as Parkinson's and Alzheimer's.

Cancer is another common genetic disease. Although cancer is a genetic disease, it is not always hereditary, meaning it can also develop from environmental causes. In the United States alone, one out of every four people dies of it, and 1.5 million cases are diagnosed each year.[8] Scientists around the world are working on developing cancer gene therapies.

Correcting Cancer

Chemotherapy (using drugs to kill cells) and radiation (using powerful beams of energy to kill cells) are the standard treatments for cancer. Unfortunately, these toxic treatments have serious side effects and often do not improve a patient's condition. Researchers have wondered whether gene therapy could offer another option.

In most cases, cancer develops after not one but several genes have been damaged. This makes gene therapy much more complex than for single-gene diseases, such as SCID or OTCD. Researchers have employed several strategies to meet this challenge in clinical trials over the last 20 years.

One strategy targets genes that control cell division, such as tumor suppressor genes. On October 16, 2003, the State FDA of China approved the sale of Gendicine, the world's first commercial gene therapy. Gendicine treats head and neck cancer by delivering a tumor suppressor gene called *P53*. In clinical trials, radiation plus weekly gene therapy caused 64 percent of tumors to disappear and another 32 percent to shrink.[9]

Glybera Goes on Sale

On November 2, 2012, the gene therapy Glybera was approved for sale throughout the European Union. Glybera treats a disease called lipoprotein lipase deficiency (LPLD), which affects one or two people out of every 1 million.[10] It causes high levels of fat in an affected person's blood. Before Glybera, the only treatment for LPLD was a diet so low in fat that most people could not follow it.

In a doctor's office, Glybera is injected into patients' thigh muscles. The therapy was developed by Doctor Daniel Gaudet's team at the University of Montreal in Canada and is sold by Netherlands gene therapy company uniQure. Glybera costs approximately $1.6 million per patient, but leader of uniQure Jörn Aldag has said this price is fair because Glybera was a long-term fix.

Another cancer gene therapy, approved in China in November 2005, uses a different strategy. Oncorine is a virus that invades cancer cells. But instead of replacing a missing human gene, the virus replicates until the cancer cell bursts, then repeats the process by infecting neighboring cells. The virus is designed to recognize cancer cells and leave healthy cells untouched. Both Gendicine and Oncorine are available only in China.

Other Cancer Therapies

Tumor suppressor therapy and killer viruses are good strategies when a patient's cancer is small or isolated. But to be effective, the vector must penetrate all of the cells. If just one cell escapes treatment, the entire tumor could grow back.

Scientists have discovered the human immune system can recognize cancer cells and kill them, just as it kills invading germs. Unfortunately, this response is not normally strong enough to prevent tumors from developing. This led scientists to explore whether gene therapy could strengthen the immune system, encouraging the body to fight its own cancer.

Scientist Malcolm Brenner's team is testing this approach for a cancer called Epstein-Barr virus associated lymphoproliferative disorder (EBV-LPD). EBV-LPD occurs in people whose immune systems are weakened by bone or organ transplants. It is the same disease from which a patient with SCID-X1, who lived in a bubble and was known as "bubble boy," died after being infected.

Brenner's team purified white cells from patients' blood and trained them to recognize EBV-LPD using gene therapy. Then the team put the cells back in the patients' bodies. Of 101 transplant patients at risk of developing the cancer, not one did. Even better, 11 of 13 patients that already had EBV-LPD were cured and remained cancer-free ten years later. Perhaps best of all, the treatment cost $6,095 per patient, much less than most other treatments developed thus far.[12]

Brenner's process used the same type of vector that killed Gelsinger. "We used to think it was too dangerous to use viruses that cause a raging infection," said David Bodine of the NIH. "But now we've realized that this incredible immune response can be turned very specifically against cancer."[13]

DNA Vaccines

Traditional vaccines expose the immune system to a weakened virus or bacterium so the body will recognize and destroy the real thing. Since 1992, scientists have been using gene therapy techniques to create DNA vaccines. DNA vaccines are plasmids that encode proteins made by germs or cancer. As those proteins are produced within the human body, a protective immune response develops.

DNA vaccines are cheap, have few side effects, and are easily administered using a gene gun. The first was approved in 2005 to protect horses against West Nile virus. Despite the human trials for many different diseases that have been conducted, DNA vaccines are not yet approved for human use.

Suicide Gene Therapy

A fourth cancer treatment technique is known as suicide gene therapy. This technique was in Phase 3 clinical trials in 2012. In this method, scientists add genes taken from viruses or bacteria into a patient's cancer cells. Then the patient takes a drug that, under normal circumstances, has no effect on the human body. Within the cancer cells, however, the newly added genes encode enzymes that activate the nontoxic drug from a harmless chemical to a toxic drug.

As with every type of gene therapy, some cancer cells do not take up the therapeutic gene. However, in the suicide method, something called a bystander effect seems to occur. Scientists are not entirely sure how it works, but the toxic drug somehow spreads from the transformed cells into neighboring cells, killing them as well. The trick is to kill all of the cancer cells without allowing healthy cells to become dead bystanders, too.

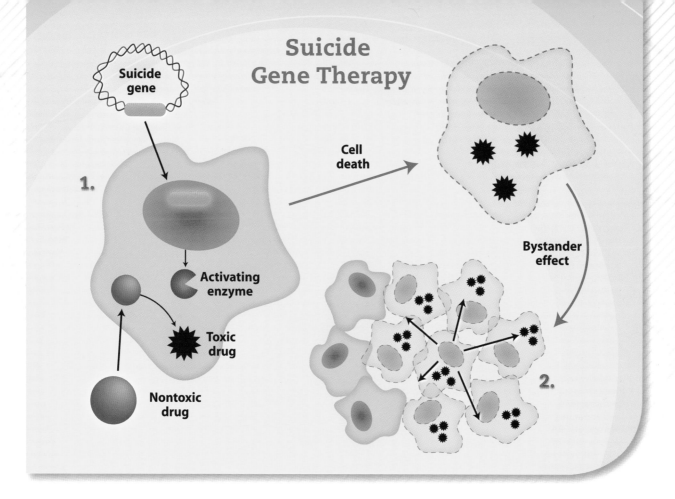

Suicide Gene Therapy

Suicide gene

1.

Activating enzyme

Toxic drug

Nontoxic drug

Cell death

Bystander effect

2.

Suicide gene therapy works better when combined with radiation or chemotherapy. In fact, combining treatments seems to be more effective with all gene therapies for cancer, likely because the disease is so complicated. But current research on cancer, and other complex diseases, is promising. It seemed gene therapy might have finally found its niche.

Prenatal Gene Therapy

Many genetic diseases impact babies' health from the day they are born. In some cases, damage caused by the disease could become permanent before possible gene therapy could take effect. But what if parents could test their unborn fetuses for genetic diseases and cure them before birth? This is the goal of prenatal gene therapy.

Prenatal gene therapy has advantages over treatment after birth. Because fetuses are small, fewer cells have to be corrected. In addition, fetuses have not yet developed immune systems, eliminating the risk of reactions to the vector used to transport therapeutic genes.

Experiments with prenatal therapy on animals began in the 1990s. The first successful treatment was in 2003. It was conducted on rats with a mutation that causes brain damage. Further successes

Doctors are able to test babies before they are born to discover whether they are afflicted with or carriers of many genetic diseases.

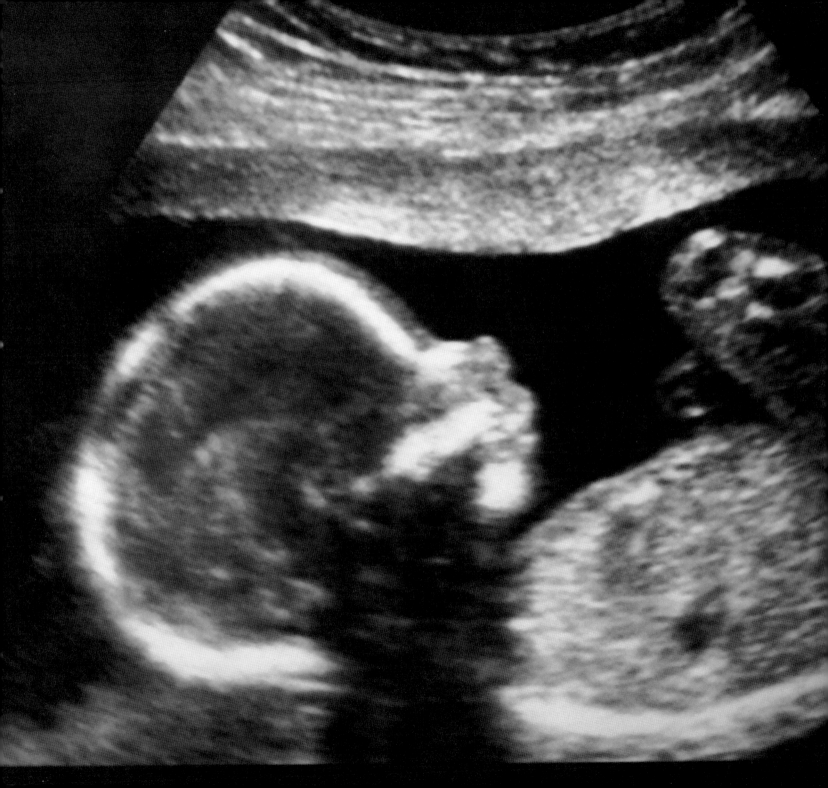

Candidate Diseases

According to the Recombinant DNA Advisory Committee (RAC), diseases that may be eligible for prenatal gene therapy should meet certain criteria. They must:

+ **Have a high risk of death**

+ **Have no effective therapies**

+ **Not cause other birth defects**

+ **Be diagnosable before birth and well understood**

+ **Have an animal model that has already been studied**

followed, showing it was possible to deliver genes almost anywhere in a fetus's body. Despite this, the RAC rejected the first proposal for a human trial in 1998, ruling that more information on risks and side effects was needed. This turned out to be a wise precaution, as further research revealed dangers of the prenatal approach.

As tiny embryos develop into entire mammals, many rounds of cell division occur. Therefore, fetal gene therapy requires vectors that permanently insert DNA into fetuses' chromosomes. However, animal tests showed prenatal gene therapy is more likely to cause cancer than gene therapy that is performed after birth. It seems the risk varies among vectors, but more safety studies are needed.

Prenatal gene therapy poses other risks to the unborn baby as well. These include birth defects and even death from infection caused by a gene therapy procedure. Prenatal gene therapy also poses risks to the mother. These include infection and potential spread of the vector from fetus to mother. If the vector does spread to the healthy mother, she could develop the same kinds of side effects observed during postnatal gene therapy in disease sufferers.

The Problem of Informed Consent

Prenatal gene therapy poses ethical problems as well as scientific ones. Before any medical procedure, patients are required to give informed consent. They must confirm they understand and accept any possible risks. Parents are legally responsible for consenting on behalf of their children. But children still have the right to refuse a procedure, including postnatal experimental trials. Unlike an older child, however, a fetus and baby cannot make decisions: its mother must choose for it and for herself.

If a fetus is diagnosed with a genetic disease, its parents currently have two options. They can accept the emotional and financial burdens of caring for the disabled child when it is born, or, where legal

A 1996 study at a US children's hospital found one-third of patients were admitted for genetic diseases and that these patients accounted for 50 percent of the hospital's yearly budget.[1] One argument for prenatal gene therapy is that it could significantly reduce this number of postnatal genetic disease patients.

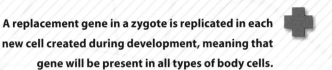

A replacement gene in a zygote is replicated in each new cell created during development, meaning that gene will be present in all types of body cells.

in the world, the mother can choose to end the pregnancy. Prenatal gene therapy would provide a third option.

To make an informed decision about a child's future, parents must understand all of the risks and benefits of each choice. For most parents, these decisions are very difficult. Adults such as Gelsinger were used in Wilson's OTCD trial for exactly this reason: Wilson felt it was wrong to pressure parents to volunteer their sick babies for the experiment.

Someday, prenatal gene therapy may offer enormous medical benefits. But these scientific and ethical challenges so far have kept it from even being tested in humans.

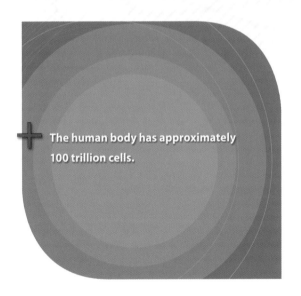

The human body has approximately 100 trillion cells.

Embryonic Gene Therapy

Getting replacement genes into every cell affected by a genetic disease is a major scientific problem. As Collins put it, the vector "has to work like a large army, spreading out and occupying a lot of territory."[2] Even in tiny unborn babies, that territory consists of thousands or even millions of cells.

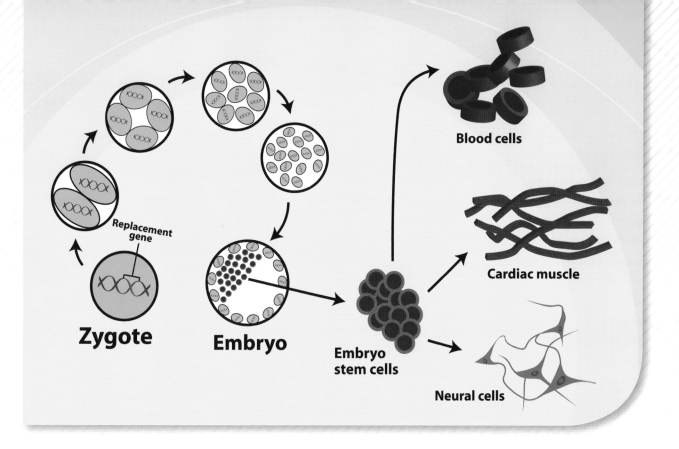

Blood cells

Cardiac muscle

Neural cells

Zygote

Replacement gene

Embryo

Embryo stem cells

But every human being begins as a single cell, or zygote. The zygote divides, creating a ball of identical cells called an embryo. As the embryo cells divide, they begin changing into all 210 cell types—each with its own job and characteristics—that make up the body. Cells with this ability to diversify are called embryonic stem cells, and they have great potential for simplifying gene therapy. If a replacement gene were added to a zygote, the stem cells would pass it to every daughter cell of every type throughout the body.

Genetically Engineered Monkey

In 2001, scientists announced the birth of ANDi, the first genetically engineered primate. ANDi is a male rhesus monkey. His name represents inserted DNA, or iDNA, spelled backward. When ANDi was just an embryo, scientists added a gene for green fluorescence protein (GFP). The GFP gene is normally found in jellyfish, where it causes a green glow. Scientists use it as an easily recognized marker that proves that successful gene transfer has occurred.

The researchers placed the transformed embryo in a female monkey, who gave birth to ANDi. The GFP gene is in every part of ANDi's body, causing him to glow in the dark. This experiment proved that a gene added to an embryo would pass to every cell in the animal's body, indicating that embryonic gene therapy is possible.

Compared with treating an entire being, transforming a zygote is simpler. For years, researchers have been using this method to successfully breed mice with recombinant DNA. There is no reason to believe it would not work in humans as well. But the possibility of using this method on human zygotes raises ethical questions that have been debated since before the development of recombinant DNA.

Postnatal gene therapy only affects somatic cells, which are the cells that make up people's bodies. It does not affect a person's germ line, which are the reproductive cells known as eggs or sperm. In other words, changes to a person's genome made by current gene therapies will not be passed on to their children.

If gene therapy were done to a zygote or embryo to be used for implanted pregnancies, however, the stem cells that became the fetus's germ line would carry the altered

Manipulating one cell before it multiplies is easier than treating the billions of cells in a developed human.

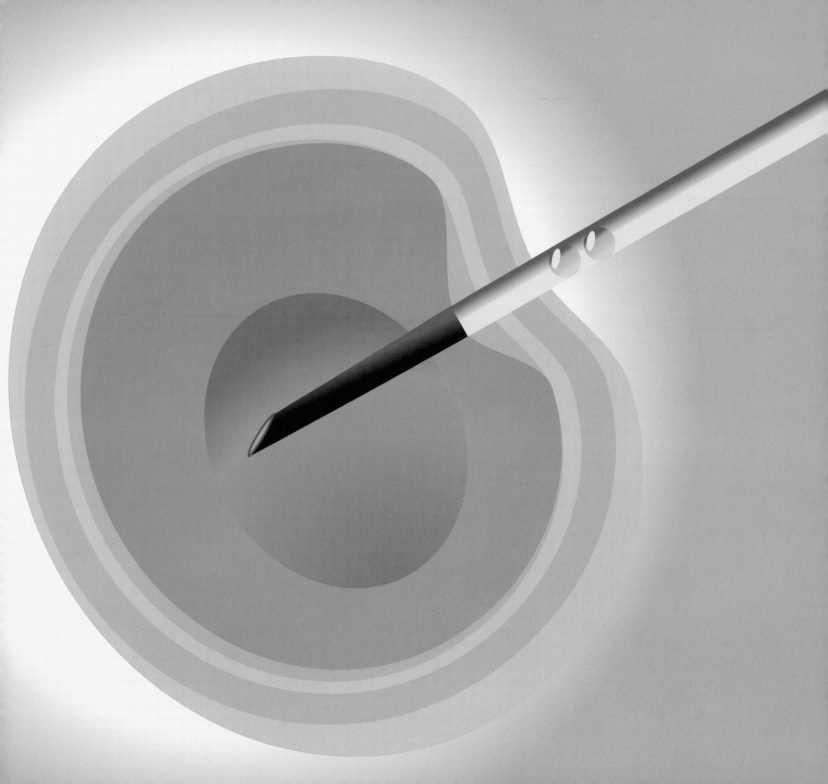

+ Adult Stem Cells

In addition to those found in embryos, a small number of stem cells are found in fully formed animals. Called adult stem cells, they are used by salamanders to regrow limbs lost due to injury. In humans, however, adult stem cells are very rare and can only create a small number of cell types. For example, 1 in every 100,000 bone marrow cells is an adult stem cell that produces red and white blood cells.[3] Recent tests show that in some cases, however, these bone marrow stem cells might also become brain, liver, or muscle cells.

Purifying enough adult stem cells to use for gene therapy is very difficult. The first attempt was made in 1991 by Doctor Claudio Bordignon's team, on patients with ADA-SCID. The patients' immune systems improved, but they still needed PEG-ADA.

genome. When the fetus grew into a person and that person went on to have children of his or her own, the change would be passed to those offspring—and to all of the offsprings' descendants as well.

Most gene therapy researchers agree that it is ethical to change genes in somatic cells due to the potential to reduce human suffering. In contrast, most researchers also believe that human germ cells (eggs and sperm) should never be a target of gene therapy. At this time, scientists are not able to accurately predict what effect germ-line changes would have on future generations. For example, if correcting disease genes creates new mutations, new diseases may result. Instead of preventing suffering, scientists might accidentally cause it.

For these reasons, the possible negative effects embryonic and germ-line gene therapy could have on future generations seem to outweigh the benefits to the individual receiving the treatment. In addition, fertility clinic doctors are able to test embryos for genetic diseases before implanting them into mothers. Therefore healthy embryos can be chosen for implantation, so there may never be a medical reason to do embryonic gene therapy.

Embryonic Stem Cell Therapy

Human embryonic stem cells were first grown in a lab in 1998. However, it was not until 2010 that the first clinical trial using them was approved. The goal was to regrow nerve cells in patients with spinal cord injuries, but the research trial was canceled in 2011 for unknown reasons. In Hungary, scientists conducted a trial for Lesch-Nyhan syndrome using stem cells taken from fetal umbilical cords. The first patient was treated at age two. Three years later, that patient had not yet begun hurting himself, meaning the therapy may have relieved the worst symptom of the disease. As of December 2012, only two stem cell trials were ongoing in the United States, both for diseases of the retina.

9

A New Age of Evolution

The history of gene therapy has shown that the human genome is more complex than scientists initially realized, and that attempts to alter it may have unexpected and deadly consequences. As a result, gene therapy may never become the magic bullet visionaries such as Anderson once hoped it would be. But patients such as Ashi and Corey have proven that in some cases, gene therapy offers a real chance for a cure.

As genetic methods for treating disease and manipulating embryos continue to improve, some people have wondered, why stop there? Technology expert Ramez Naam addressed this question:

Once you accept the idea of genetically altering an embryo to remove a gene that might cause cancer, it's not a far step to adding a gene that reduces the risk of cancer. Once you accept adding

As gene therapy technologies improve and research continues, altering genetic traits to create enhanced humans is under debate.

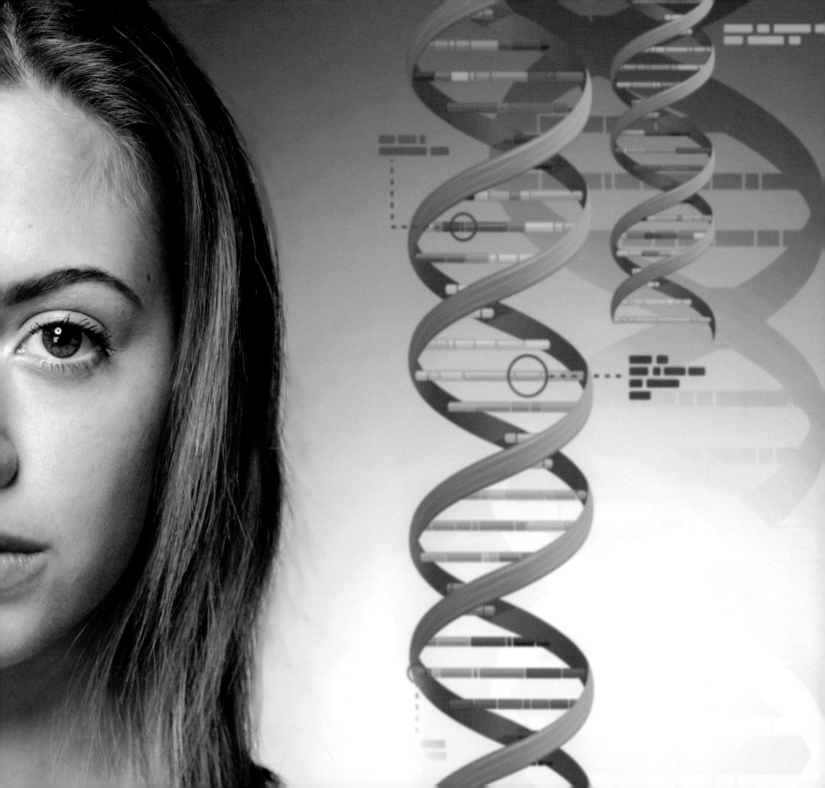

a gene that reduces the risk of a disease, a gene that increases youthful life span and thus reduces the risk of many diseases seems more reasonable. Once society is comfortable with splicing in genes to reduce a child's risk of obesity and thus stave off heart disease and diabetes, choosing genes that promote good looks or intelligence doesn't seem so shocking.[1]

The idea of parents choosing desirable traits for their children is shocking to 80 percent of Americans, but 63 percent of people in India and 83 percent of those in Thailand are in favor of it.[2] And experiments using animal embryos show that gene therapy for human enhancement is becoming a real possibility.

Improving the Body

PEPCK-C is a gene with a job that is not well understood. To figure out its role in muscles, Doctor Richard Hanson's team inserted an extra copy of the gene into mouse embryos. After birth, these mice ate 60 percent more food than average mice without gaining weight. On a treadmill, the mice with the extra gene ran 66 feet (20 m) per minute for 3.7 miles

Many people, including James Watson, argue gene therapy for beauty is not much different than today's plastic surgery.

(6 km) before becoming exhausted, while normal mice could only run 0.1 miles (0.2 km) at this pace.[3]

Hanson's team was not the first to create mighty mice. In 1998, when University of Pennsylvania researcher Lee Sweeney was studying muscle loss caused by aging, he accidently produced mice that were 30 percent stronger than normal.[4] When the results were revealed, Sweeney was swamped with calls from athletes wanting the technology.

Gene doping is defined as the use of genes to enhance athletic ability. Concerns that athletes could use it to cheat were raised during the 2012 London Olympics. Compared to drugs such as steroids, gene doping would be very hard to detect.

And it is not only athletes who might be interested. "Just say you'd like your pectoralis muscles to be a little larger because you want to look a little better at the beach,"

The End of Old Age?

In the late 1980s, researchers discovered a strain of worms that lived twice as long as normal members of the species. Their increased lifespan was due to a mutation in a single gene. Since then, dozens of genes have been found that extend the lifespan of worms, fruit flies, and mice. Humans share many of these genes.

However, it is unlikely that gene therapy for human aging will be tested any time soon. One reason is because those long-lived mice have experienced side effects such as stunted growth and infertility. But the research has implications beyond its immediate results. In the words of biologist Michael Rose, who worked on the fruit fly project, "Aging . . . is a genetic problem, and you can solve it."[5]

said Sweeney. "[Take] a few injections of the virus, and a month later while you're watching television, your muscles have gotten bigger."[6]

Enhancing the Mind

In the late 1990s, scientist Joe Tsien's research team was studying brain cell connections and their role in memory. The team focused their research on a protein called NR2B.

The researchers added an extra copy of the *NR2B* gene to mouse embryos. When the mice were born, their brains had twice as much NR2B protein as normal. Tsien's group tested the mice using a Morris water maze, which is set in a circular pool filled with murky water. Hidden in the maze is a platform, invisible just below the water. Mice do not like being wet, so they swim around the maze until they find the platform. The genetically enhanced mice found the platform faster than regular mice. In a second test, Tsien removed the platform and put the mice back in the maze. Compared to regular test subjects, the enhanced mice spent more time swimming in the area where the platform had been, indicating that they remembered its location.

Researchers named these mice "Doogie" after the teenaged doctor prodigy on a popular 1990s television show called *Doogie Howser, M.D.* Someday, Doogie mice may provide the key to treating human memory diseases. "Understanding the molecular basis of learning and memory is so important

because what we learn and what we remember determine largely who we are," Tsien said. "Memory, not merely facial and physical appearance, defines an individual, as everyone who has known someone with Alzheimer's disease understands all too well."[7]

But what would happen if healthy people had gene therapy for *NR2B*? Geneticist Tim Tully believes that memory enhancing treatments could become "lifestyle drugs," used by "anyone interested in learning a second language, in playing a musical instrument, or in studying for an exam."[8] As with gene doping for athletes, people who received such treatments could have a major advantage over people who did not. And Tsien knows that people are interested in these types of treatments, even though they are not yet possible. "Everyone I have encountered since the publication of our results has wanted to know whether the findings mean we will soon be able to genetically engineer smarter children or devise pills that will make everyone a genius," he said. "The short answer is no—and would we even want to?"[9]

The New Eugenics?

Gene therapy is not the first technology that has given people the power to direct humanity's evolution. In the early 1900s, as Mendel's heredity and Darwin's theory of evolution became accepted, the eugenics movement was born. The goal of the movement was to create a perceived improvement to the human population by controlling breeding. Its tool was sterilization, a surgery that disables or removes a person's reproductive organs.

More than 30 US states had eugenics laws.[10] These laws gave their governments the right to sterilize different types of "socially inadequate individuals," most of whom were considered "insane and feeble-minded." Between 1907 and January 1, 1921, 3,233 US citizens were forcibly sterilized.[11]

Before it was over, the eugenics movement spread to both Canada and Nazi Germany. Today, many people believe using gene therapy to treat disease, and especially for enhancement, is just as ethically wrong as the eugenics movement. Gilbert Meilander, a member of the President's Council on Bioethics, is firmly opposed to human gene therapy. In 2001, he wrote:

> We have entered a new era of eugenics. That science which attempts to improve the inherited characteristics of the species and which had gone so suddenly out of fashion after World War II and the Nazi doctors now climbs steadily back toward respectability.[12]

Collins disagrees with this viewpoint. "To say that genetic engineering is unacceptable across the board because of its potential for creating some ethical dilemmas is the most unethical stance of all," he said. He continued,

> What [the technology] does do is require us to assume some responsibility for deciding which kinds of genetic engineering are, in fact, consistent with that mandate to heal the sick, and which kinds are putting us in a troubling direction where we'd best not go.[13]

"Once you have a way in which you can improve our children, no one can stop it. It would be stupid not to use it, because someone else will. . . . Those parents who enhance their children, then their children are going to be the ones who dominate the world."[14]

—James Watson

Adam and Molly Nash

Molly Nash had Fanconi anemia, a genetic disease that prevents the body from making bone marrow. Bone marrow transplants from siblings are 85 percent successful, but Molly did not have a sibling.[15] Using in vitro fertilization, where sperm fertilizes an egg outside the body, Molly's parents had a second child, named Adam. The child's genome was chosen so his bone marrow was a perfect match for Molly. A few weeks after his birth on August 29, 2000, stem cells from Adam's umbilical cord were given to Molly. Both children survived. This was the first time genetic methods were used to choose a child's characteristics.

Humanity's Future

While ethical debates continue, the reality is that it is often hard to stop technology. And banning the technology likely would not stop its advancement or use, just as making drugs illegal has not prevented people from taking them. Instead, a ban would make gene therapy more expensive. As the price for enhancements rose, only wealthy people would be able to afford them. Wealthy parents could upgrade their children's bodies and brains, widening existing gaps between social and economic groups. Because of this, some argue the best approach is to level the playing field by making genetic enhancements as cheaply and widely available as possible.

While many believe genetic enhancement is ethically questionable and not a practical necessity, Naam considers

it a positive and inevitable forward step. "The drive to alter and improve on ourselves is a fundamental part of who we humans are," he said. Naam continued,

> In just a few decades, we've gone from the first tinkering with human genes to the discovery of dozens of techniques that could alter the human genome in very precise ways. Those techniques give us the power to cure diseases or to enhance and sculpt our bodies. This new control over our genes promises to enhance our quality of life as dramatically as the medical discoveries of the past century.[16]

Many scientific and ethical questions must be resolved before gene therapy research can deliver on such promises. But many researchers, geneticists, and doctors are awed by the possibilities. Continued research, advancing technology, and a continued passion for discovery promise to further reveal the marvels of genetics in the future.

Timeline

1865

Gregor Mendel publishes his study of inheritance patterns in pea plants, launching the science of genetics.

1928

Fred Griffith discovers that genetic characteristics can be exchanged between individual bacteria.

1953

James Watson and Francis Crick describe the double helix structure of DNA.

1969

Werner Arber, Daniel Nathans, and Hamilton Smith discover restriction enzymes, making recombinant DNA research possible.

1969

Jonathan Beckwith becomes the first person to isolate a single gene out of an entire genome.

1990

On September 14, Ashanti (Ashi) DeSilva becomes the first patient in the first official human gene therapy trial, for ADA-SCID.

1991

The first gene therapy trial that also uses stem cells is attempted but is only partly successful.

1998

Craig Venter tells Francis Collins that Celera Genomics will shotgun sequence the entire human genome, and do it more quickly than HGP.

1999

On September 17, Jesse Gelsinger becomes the first person to die from gene therapy.

2000

On June 26, Francis Collins and Craig Venter present the first draft of the complete human genome sequence at a White House ceremony.

1970

Stanfield Rogers and colleagues perform the first human gene therapy experiment when they infect two girls with a natural rabbit virus, but it is unsuccessful.

1974

Paul Berg and colleagues recommend that scientists be cautious when planning experiments that use recombinant DNA technology.

1980

Martin Cline defies regulatory committees and conducts the first human gene therapy trial using recombinant DNA. The trial fails, and Cline's career is destroyed.

1984

Theodore Friedmann's team adds an *HPRT* gene to cells from a Lesch-Nyhan patient in the first successful preclinical gene therapy experiment using recombinant DNA.

1990

The National Institutes of Health launches the Human Genome Project.

2002

Researchers discover patients in a gene therapy trial for SCID-X1 have developed cancer.

2003

Fetal rats, models for a human brain disease, become the first animals successfully treated with prenatal gene therapy.

2003

On October 16, the State Food and Drug Administration of China approves the sale of Gendicine, the world's first commercial gene therapy.

2012

On July 9, President Barack Obama signs the FDA Safety and Innovation Act, which includes funding for the study of rare and neglected diseases.

2012

In November, the 1000 Genomes Project publishes its study of genetic variation in 1,092 complete human genomes, with plans to add 1,500 more.

Glossary

clinical trial

An experiment using living humans that tests the safety and effectiveness of new medical treatments.

dominant

A genetic trait or mutation that affects an individual when one or two copies are present in the genome.

enzyme

A protein that causes a specific chemical change in all parts of the body. All bodily functions, such as digestion and blood clotting, require enzymes. Enzymes exist in every organ and cell in the body.

gene patent

Legal ownership of a DNA sequence granting the sole right to make, use, or sell it or products based on it.

genome

The complete set of genetic information for an individual or species.

germ line

Cells in the human body (eggs or sperm) that are used to create offspring, carrying an individual's genetic traits into the next generation.

informed consent

A patient's understanding and acceptance of the risks involved in a medical treatment such as gene therapy. It is required before doctors or scientists can conduct a treatment.

mutation

A change in the DNA sequence of a gene.

preclinical trial

Research done on isolated cells or model animal species proving the safety and effectiveness of a technique before it is tested on humans.

prenatal gene therapy

Gene therapy done to an embryo or fetus before its birth.

recessive

A genetic trait or mutation that only affects an individual when two copies are present in the genome.

recombinant DNA

A piece of DNA that is created in a lab and contains sequences from more than one species, or sequences from the same species that are not normally joined together in the genome.

sequencing

Determining the exact order of nitrogen bases A, G, C, and T in a piece of DNA.

somatic line

Cells that are not passed to, or involved in, creating offspring (for example, skin or lung cells).

transform

To insert foreign or replacement genes into a living cell, animal, or human.

tumor suppressor gene

A gene that slows down or prevents cell division in cancer tumors.

vaccine

A treatment that teaches the human immune system to recognize invading bacteria, viruses, or cancer cells.

vector

A biological, chemical, or physical agent used for delivering foreign or replacement genes into living cells or individuals.

Additional Resources

Selected Bibliography

Duncan, David Ewing. *Masterminds: Genius, DNA, and the Quest to Rewrite Life*. New York: Harper, 2006. Print.

Lewis, Ricki. *The Forever Fix: Gene Therapy and the Boy Who Saved It*. New York: St. Martin's, 2012. Print.

Sheridan, Cormac. "Gene Therapy Finds Its Niche." *Nature Biotechnology* 29.2 (2011): 121–28. Print.

Turnpenny, Peter D., and Sian Ellard. *Emery's Elements of Medical Genetics*. 14 ed. Philadelphia: Elsevier, 2012. Print.

Further Readings

Canini, Mikko. *Genetic Engineering*. Farmington Hills, MI: Greenhaven, 2006. Print.

Simpson, Kathleen. *Genetics: From DNA to Designer Dogs*. Washington, DC: National Geographic, 2008. Print.

Web Sites

To learn more about gene therapy, visit ABDO Publishing Company online at **www.abdopublishing.com.** Web sites about gene therapy are featured on our Book Links page. These links are routinely monitored and updated to provide the most current information available.

For More Information

National Human Genome Research Institute

National Institutes of Health, Building 31, Room 4B09
31 Center Drive, MSC 2152, 9000 Rockville Pike
Bethesda, MD 20892-2152
301-402-0911
http://www.genome.gov

The National Human Genome Research Institute is the division of the National Institutes of Health that studies the human genome and the role of DNA in disease.

National Organization for Rare Disorders

55 Kenosia Avenue
Danbury, CT 06810
800-999-6673
http://www.rarediseases.org

The National Organization for Rare Disorders is a nonprofit organization devoted to research and education on rare disorders and their treatment.

Recombinant DNA Advisory Committee

6705 Rockledge Drive, Suite 750, MSC 7985
Bethesda, MD 20892-7985
301-496-9838
http://oba.od.nih.gov/rdna_rac/rac_about.html

The Recombinant DNA Advisory Committee was created in 1974 to regulate recombinant DNA research, including gene therapy.

Source Notes

Chapter 1. The Boy Who Could Not See

1. Ricki Lewis. *The Forever Fix: Gene Therapy and the Boy Who Saved It*. New York: St. Martin's, 2012. Print. 7.

2. Ibid. 20.

3. G. Le Meur, et al. "Restoration of Vision in RPE65-Deficient Briard Dogs Using an AAV Serotype 4 Vector That Specifically Targets the Retinal Pigmented Epithelium." *Gene Therapy* 14.4 (2006): 292. Print.

4. Xue Cai, Shannon M. Conley, and Muna I. Naash. "RPE65: Role in the Visual Cycle, Human Retinal Disease, and Gene Therapy." *Ophthalmic Genetics* 30.2 (2009): 58. Print.

5. Ricki Lewis. *The Forever Fix: Gene Therapy and the Boy Who Saved It*. New York: St. Martin's, 2012. Print. 15.

6. Ibid. 164.

7. Ibid. 246.

8. Ibid. 254.

9. Jocelyn Kaiser. "Gene Therapy in a New Light." *Smithsonian. com*. Smithsonian Media, Jan. 2009. Web. 1 May 2013.

10. Ricki Lewis. *The Forever Fix: Gene Therapy and the Boy Who Saved It*. New York: St. Martin's, 2012. Print. lx.

11. CBS News. "Gene Therapy Helps Blind Boy See." *CBS News*. CBS Interactive, 26 Oct. 2009. Web. 1 May 2013.

12. "Latest Update: Childhood Rediscovered: Gene Therapy Restores Vision for 9-Year Old With LCA." *Foundation Fighting Blindness*. Foundation Fighting Blindness, 2012. Web. 1 May 2013.

Chapter 2. Disease and the Double Helix

1. Peter D. Turnpenny and Sian Ellard. *Emery's Elements of Medical Genetics*. 14 ed. Philadelphia, PA: Elsevier, 2012. Print. 15.

2. Gelehrter, Thomas D., Francis S. Collins, and David Ginsburg. "Gene Therapy." *Principles of Medical Genetics*. 2nd ed. Baltimore: Williams & Wilkins, 1998. Print. 311–328.

Chapter 3. Recombinant DNA

1. Richard Preston. "An Error in the Code." *The New Yorker*. Condé Nast, 13 Aug. 2007. Web. 1 May 2013.

2. David Ewing Duncan. *Masterminds: Genius, DNA, and the Quest to Rewrite Life*. New York: Harper, 2006. Print. 212.

3. Ibid. 212–213.

4. Ibid. 222.

5. Ibid. 215, 224.

6. Ricki Lewis. *The Forever Fix: Gene Therapy and the Boy Who Saved It*. New York: St. Martin's, 2012. Print. 45.

Chapter 4. The Human Genome Project: Hunting Genes

1. David Ewing Duncan. *Masterminds: Genius, DNA, and the Quest to Rewrite Life*. New York: Harper, 2006. Print. 99.

2. Ibid. 101.

3. Ibid.

4. Francis S. Collins and Anna D. Baker. "Mapping the Cancer Gene (pdf)." *UCLA Department of Molecular, Cell, and Developmental Biology*. Scientific American, Mar. 2007. Web. 1 May 2013.

5. "About the DPD." *DNA Patent Database*. Kennedy Institute of Ethics, Georgetown University, 18 June 2012. Web. 1 May 2013.

6. Richard Preston. "The Genome Warrior." *The New Yorker*. Condé Nast, 12 June 2000. Web. 1 May 2013.

7. Ibid.

8. "An Overview of the Human Genome Project." *National Human Genome Research Institute*. National Institutes of Health, 8 Nov. 2012. Web. 1 May 2013.

9. Peter D. Turnpenny and Sian Ellard. *Emery's Elements of Medical Genetics*. 14 ed. Philadelphia: Elsevier, 2012. Print. 73.

10. David Ewing Duncan. *Masterminds: Genius, DNA, and the Quest to Rewrite Life*. New York: Harper, 2006. Print. 102.

11. The 1000 Genomes Project Consortium. "An Integrated Map of Genetic Variation From 1,092 Human Genomes." *Nature* 491.7422 (2012): 56. Print.

12. Alok Jha. "Genomes Project Publishes Inventory of Human Genetic Variation." *The Guardian*. Guardian News and Media, 31 Oct. 2012. Web. 1 May 2013.

13. Ricki Lewis. *The Forever Fix: Gene Therapy and the Boy Who Saved It*. New York: St. Martin's, 2012. Print. 19.

14. The 1000 Genomes Project Consortium. "An Integrated Map of Genetic Variation From 1,092 Human Genomes." *Nature* 491.7422 (2012): 57, 60. Print.

15. "An Overview of the Human Genome Project." *National Human Genome Research Institute*. National Institutes of Health, 8 Nov. 2012. Web. 1 May 2013.

Chapter 5. Fever Dreams and Rude Awakenings

1. Ricki Lewis. *The Forever Fix: Gene Therapy and the Boy Who Saved It*. New York: St. Martin's, 2012. Print. 85.

2. Ibid. 72.

3. Craig A. Mullen, et al. "Molecular Analysis of T Lymphocyte-Directed Gene Therapy for Adenosine Deaminase Deficiency: Long-Term Expression in Vivo of Genes Introduced With a Retroviral Vector." *Human Gene Therapy* 7 (1996): 1123. Print.

4. Ricki Lewis. *The Forever Fix: Gene Therapy and the Boy Who Saved It*. New York: St. Martin's, 2012. Print. 88.

5. Linda L. McCabe and Edward R. B. McCabe. *DNA: Promise and Peril*. Berkeley: U of California P, 2008. Print. 243.

6. Donald B. Kohn and Fabio Condotti. "Gene Therapy Fulfilling Its Promise." *New England Journal of Medicine* 360.5 (2009): 519. Print.

7. Ricki Lewis. *The Forever Fix: Gene Therapy and the Boy Who Saved It*. New York: St. Martin's, 2012. Print. 37.

8. Francis S. Collins. *The Language of Life: DNA and the Revolution in Personalized Medicine*. New York: Harper, 2010. Print. 257.

9. Sheryl Gay Stolberg. "Youth's Death Shakes New Field of Gene Experiments on Humans." *New York Times*. New York Times, 27 Jan. 2000. Web. 1 May 2013.

10. Jocelyn Kaiser. "Gene Therapy in a New Light." *Smithsonian.com*. Smithsonian Media, Jan. 2009. Web. 1 May 2013.

11. Ricki Lewis. *The Forever Fix: Gene Therapy and the Boy Who Saved It*. New York: St. Martin's, 2012. Print. 97.

12. Cormac Sheridan. "Gene Therapy Finds Its Niche." *Nature Biotechnology* 29.2 (2011): 121. Print.

Chapter 6. New Vectors

1. Bruce L. Levine, et al. "Gene Transfer in Humans Using a Conditionally Replicating Lentiviral Vector." *Proceedings of the National Academy of Science* 103.46 (2006): 17372. Print.

2. Ricki Lewis. *The Forever Fix: Gene Therapy and the Boy Who Saved It*. New York: St. Martin's, 2012. Print. 128.

3. Nathalie Cartier, et al. "Hematopoietic Stem Cell Gene Therapy With a Lentiviral Vector in X-Linked Adrenoleukodystrophy." *Science* 326.5954 (2009): 818–821. Print.

4. Michael Winerip. "Fighting for Jacob." *New York Times*. New York Times, 6 Dec. 1998. Web. 1 May 2013.

5. Ibid.

6. Ibid.

7. Ricki Lewis. *The Forever Fix: Gene Therapy and the Boy Who Saved It.* New York: St. Martin's, 2012. Print. 216.

8. Charles Lu, et al. "Phase I Clinical Trial of Systemically Administered USC2(FUS1)-Nanoparticles Mediating Functional Gene Transfer in Humans." *PLoS ONE* 7.4 (2012): 4. Print.

9. A. D. Kandasamy, et al. "Adiponectin Gene Therapy Ameliorates High-Fat, High-Sucrose Diet-Induced Metabolic Perturbations in Mice." *Nutrition and Diabetes* 2 (2012): 2, 4. Print.

Chapter 7. From Unicorns to Horses

1. Ricki Lewis. *The Forever Fix: Gene Therapy and the Boy Who Saved It.* New York: St. Martin's, 2012. Print. 21.

2. Ricki Lewis. "Rare Diseases: 5 Recent Reasons to Cheer." *Scientific American.* Scientific American/Nature America, 29 July 2012. Web. 1 May 2013.

3. "Research Grant Policy." *NORD.* National Organization for Rare Disorders, 2013. Web. 1 May 2013.

4. Ricki Lewis. *The Forever Fix: Gene Therapy and the Boy Who Saved It.* New York: St. Martin's, 2012. Print. 166.

5. "NIH Announces New Program to Develop Therapeutics for Rare and Neglected Diseases." *National Human Genome Research Institute: NIH News.* National Institute of Health, 20 May 2009. Web. 1 May 2013.

6. Ramez Naam. *More Than Human: Embracing the Promise of Biological Enhancement.* New York: Broadway, 2005. Print. 63.

7. Ricki Lewis. "Rare Diseases: 5 Recent Reasons to Cheer." *Scientific American.* Scientific American, 29 July 2012. Web. 1 May 2013.

8. Nikiforos Ballian, Bert W. O'Malley Jr., and F. Charles Brunicardi. "Suicide Gene Therapy." *Gene and Cell Therapy: Therapeutic Mechanisms and Strategies.* Ed. Nancy Smith Templeton. 3rd ed. Boca Raton, FL: Taylor & Francis, 2009. Print. 539.

9. Sue Pearson, Hepeng Jia, and Keiko Kandachi. "China Approves First Gene Therapy." *Nature Biotechnology* 22.1 (2004): 3. Print.

10. Cormac Sheridan. "Gene Therapy Finds Its Niche." *Nature Biotechnology* 29.2 (2011): 124. Print.

11. Jenny Hope. "Drug to Fix Faulty DNA Gets Go-Ahead in Landmark Move That May Alter Medicine Forever." *Mail Online.* Associated Newspapers, 2 Nov. 2012. Web. 1 May 2013.

12. Helen E. Heslop, et al. "Long-Term Outcome of EBY-Specific T-Cell Infusions to Prevent or Treat EBY-Related Lymphoproliferative Disease in Transplant Recipients." *Blood* 115.5 (2010): 929–933. Print.

13. Jill Neimark. "The Second Coming of Gene Therapy." *Discover.* Kalmbach Publishing, 2 Sep. 2009. Web. 1 May 2013.

Chapter 8. Prenatal Gene Therapy

1. Shawn E. McCandless, Jeanne W. Brunger, and Suzanne B. Cassidy. "The Burden of Genetic Disease on Inpatient Care in a Children's Hospital." *American Journal of Human Genetics* 74.1 (Jan. 2004). *PMC: Library of Medicine, National Institutes of Health.* Web. 1 May 2013.

2. Francis S. Collins. *The Language of Life: DNA and the Revolution in Personalized Medicine.* New York: HarperCollins, 2010. Print. 34.

3. "Stem Cell Information: Regenerative Medicine; 5. Hematopoietic Stem Cells." *National Institutes of Health.* US Department of Health & Human Services, 20 Jan. 2011. Web. 1 May 2013.

Chapter 9. A New Age of Evolution

1. Ramez Naam. *More Than Human: Embracing the Promise of Biological Enhancement*. New York: Broadway, 2005. Print. 149.

2. Ibid. 58.

3. Parvin Hakimi, et al. "Overexpression of the Cytosolic Form of Phosphoenolpyruvate Carboxykinase (GTP) in Skeletal Muscle Repatterns Energy Metabolism in the Mouse." *Journal of Biological Chemistry* 282.45 (2007): 32845–32849. Print.

4. Steve Connor. "The Cheat Gene." *The Independent*. Independent.co.uk, 23 Aug. 2012. Web. 1 May 2013.

5. Ramez Naam. *More Than Human: Embracing the Promise of Biological Enhancement*. New York: Broadway, 2005. Print. 83, 111.

6. Ibid. 27.

7. Joe Z. Tsien. "Building a Brainier Mouse." *Scientific American* Apr. 2000: 62–63. Print.

8. Ramez Naam. *More Than Human: Embracing the Promise of Biological Enhancement*. New York: Broadway, 2005. Print. 49.

9. Joe Z. Tsien. "Building a Brainier Mouse." *Scientific American* Apr. 2000: 67. Print.

10. Paul A. Lombardo, ed. *A Century of Eugenics in America*. Bloomington, IN: Indiana UP, 2011. *Google Book Search*. Web. 1 May 2013.

11. Harry H. Laughlin. *Eugenical Sterilization in the United States*. Chicago: Psychopathic Laboratory of the Municipal Court of Chicago, 1922. *DNA Patent Database*. Web. 1 May 2013.

12. Ramez Naam. *More Than Human: Embracing the Promise of Biological Enhancement*. New York: Broadway, 2005. Print. 166.

13. David Ewing Duncan. *Masterminds: Genius, DNA, and the Quest to Rewrite Life*. New York: Harper, 2006. Print. 106.

14. Steven Potter. *Designer Genes: A New Era in the Evolution of Man*. New York: Random, 2010. Print. 174.

15. Gerard Magill. "Science, Ethics, and Policy: Relating Human Genomics to Embryonic Stem-Cell Research and Therapeutic Cloning." *Genetics and Ethics: An Interdisciplinary Study*. Ed. Gerard Magill. Saint Louis: Saint Louis UP, 2004. Print. 254–255.

16. Ramez Naam. *More Than Human: Embracing the Promise of Biological Enhancement*. New York: Broadway, 2005. Print. 41.

Index

About the Author

L. E. Carmichael never outgrew that stage of childhood when nothing was more fun than amazing her friends (and correcting her teachers!) with a stockpile of weird and wonderful facts. Her sense of wonder came in handy during her career as a scientist. In 2006, she received the Governor General's Medal for her PhD thesis, *Ecological Genetics of Northern Wolves and Arctic Foxes*. These days, Carmichael writes for kids, teens, and occasionally adults. Her work has appeared in magazines such as *Dig* and *Highlights for Children*, and she has published six previous science books.

About the Consultant

Nathaniel Comfort, PhD, is an associate professor at the Institute of the History of Medicine at the John Hopkins University in Maryland. His interests and areas of expertise include the history of genetics and biomedicine, and he has authored several journal articles and books on the topic. His published books include *The Science of Human Perfection: How Genes Became the Heart of American Medicine* (2012) and *The Tangled Field: Barbara McClintock's Search for the Patterns of Genetic Control* (2001), as well as the edited volume, *The Panda's Black Box: Opening Up the Intelligent Design Controversy* (2009).